We all ha
tell t this happens to be
mine "SO FAN"...
Best,
Jiffy E. Mayold

Power *and* Pinstripes

Power *and* Pinstripes

My Years Training the New York Yankees

Jeff Mangold with Peter Botte

TRIUMPH
BOOKS

Library of Congress Cataloging-in-Publication Data

Names: Mangold, Jeff, author. | Botte, Peter, author.
Title: Power and pinstripes : my years training the New York Yankees / Jeff Mangold with Peter Botte.
Description: Chicago, Illinois : Triumph Books, [2021] | Includes bibliographical references.
Identifiers: LCCN 2021058754 | ISBN 9781629378725 (hardcover)
Subjects: LCSH: Mangold, Jeff. | New York Yankees (Baseball team)—History. | New York Yankees (Baseball team)—Anecdotes. | Athletic trainers—New York (State)—New York—Biography. | Baseball—United States—History.
Classification: LCC GV875.N4 .M34 2021 | DDC 796.092 [B]—dc23
LC record available at https://lccn.loc.gov/2021058754

This book is available in quantity at special discounts for your group or organization. For further information, contact:

Triumph Books LLC
814 North Franklin Street
Chicago, Illinois 60610
(312) 337-0747
www.triumphbooks.com

Printed in U.S.A.
ISBN: 978-1-62937-872-5
Design by Patricia Frey
Photos courtesy of Jeff Mangold unless otherwise indicated

For my wife, Gale, and our children, Sean, Jaime, and Jesse—the greatest team ever assembled.

Contents

Foreword

ONE OF THE MANY PEOPLE I ALWAYS LIKE TO CREDIT FOR THE
success I had in my career and the success we had with the New
York Yankees was Jeff Mangold. He was hired as our strength and
conditioning coach in 1998, and we won three straight World Series
championships in his first three seasons with the team. But it was
so much more than that. I always felt like we had a special, personal
relationship that helped me both as a player and as a person. The
thing that I liked about Jeff right away was that he was always
available to me.

He was always one of those people trying to put us as a team in
a position to shine. I always liked to take advantage of his presence
on the team. Stretching and doing those type of exercises to keep
your body in shape are the obvious things that every strength and
conditioning coach does. With Jeff it always went beyond that—
whether it was the things he did to keep things loose and fun for
the players or the little pushes he would always provide to keep us
healthy and hungry. I enjoyed a great personal relationship with him
and his family. It was very special to me.

Maintaining my body always was important to me throughout my career. Whether I was in Single A or the major leagues, I always wanted to make sure that I was available to be on the field. I wanted to be stretched so that I was strong and able to do my job to the best of my ability. As you know by now, I always liked to shag fly balls during batting practice to help with my conditioning, and that was something that Jeff did with me quite often. But for me to do that, I had to make sure I was stretched out. I had to make sure that I worked on my shoulder, elbow, upper-body, and lower-body programs that Jeff provided. It allowed me to stay in shape all the way into the playoffs and the World Series. Any time I needed Jeff, he was there, and that's what I always appreciated about our coaches, trainers, and strength and conditioning coaches.

We connected from the start of his time with the team. When I first met Jeff, he told me a story of when he lived in Iowa, he used to work out at Briar Cliff College (now a university) in Sioux City, and there were several basketball players there who were from Panama, my home country. It was like an instant connection for me when he talked about guys like Mario Butler, Rolando Frazer, Tito Malcolm, and Eddie Warren. It was important for me. Any time you meet someone who is working with you and they have some type of bond with people from your home country, it is an opening there for your relationship. It made it easier to connect with Jeff, knowing that he understood athletes from where I came from.

From the beginning I always took my work with Jeff seriously, but I never felt the need to try to influence the other players to take it seriously, too. Jeff always reminded us how important it was, but we were a group of players who always motivated ourselves and each other. We just wanted the team to be the best it could be. And we knew those were all the little things that we needed to do to get better. So there definitely was enough motivation already, and I feel like all the guys led by that example. But then also we had Jeff, our strength and conditioning coordinator, there to push us.

Working with him was fun, too. We made it fun, and Jeff made it fun. That was a big part of why it worked so well. Guys never complained about having to do that work. We used these big rubber bands to stretch, and guys threw them at each other and shot them like missiles, flicking them up in the air. The reliever group—myself, Ramiro Mendoza, and Jeff Nelson—had a great time with Jeff, teasing each other, but when it came time to do our conditioning work at the end of batting practice, we would get it done.

We did different conditioning sets, and Jeff tried to do something different with us every other day, so we would not get stale. Jeff used to do one drill with us, where he threw us touchdown passes. We got in our running by going out for a pass like a receiver in football, and Jeff was the quarterback. We would each have a baseball in our gloves and hand it to Jeff, and he would throw us the ball as we sprinted down the field 30 or 40 yards. We did this out in the outfield, and that was always a great time. In addition to shagging the fly balls in the outfield during BP, this was another fun thing that we would do to get in some running. You could tell Jeff played sports growing up. You could tell he was a good athlete, too. We would put on a show. People in the stands would be like, "Wow." Jeff was very accurate throwing the ball. Mike Mussina was very athletic too and really liked to do that drill. Everybody would be making these great catches on the run down the field. Those were the kinds of things that made training enjoyable for us. It was conditioning because we were running, but it was fun, too. We had some competitive guys who wanted to outdo each other. That's what Jeff was good about.

We wanted to do things that were a little different to keep it fresh while also doing the job. That was important because it's such a long season. You want to make sure that everybody was interested and motivated to do their work, and doing things like that football drill kept it interesting for the guys to do whatever we needed to do. It was so important.

Because it was a long season, there were stretches of time occasionally when I would go a little while without lifting. But I liked that Jeff knew when to give us space and when to push us. He knew the right time to say, "Listen, Mariano, let's get in the gym and do some leg squats or other exercises" to help me maintain my leg strength, my lower body, my abs, my core. We trusted him so much that we always listened when Jeff told us what we needed to do to stay in the best possible shape for the team. Sometimes you need the coaches or the strength trainers to tell you something they are noticing—even if it's just a little thing. You appreciate people like that who really take care of you.

Another thing that helped Jeff's relationships was he had a very good, dry sense of humor, and we would tease each other all the time. He took his job seriously, but he wasn't afraid to make jokes with all the players—even the stars of the team—and that was another important aspect about the relationship. You have to be able to laugh over the course of the season. I would try to get other teammates involved, and we would embarrass Jeff sometimes with a joke because I knew he could take it and would have a good sense of humor about it. I would say, "What are you doing to us, Mangold? Are you crazy?" And the guys would laugh, and that was always important. It almost would look like we were arguing sometimes, but it was always as a joke.

With baseball being such a long season, you had to make the best out of grinding out each day. On that team we did exactly that. If you're not having fun on a team like that with as much success as we had, what's the point, right? We knew how to have a good time, but when it was time to be serious, we knew how to do that, too.

Jeff also is a strong man of faith just like my family and I are, and that was another strong connection with us. We needed to have that. As a Christian I believed it was a big part of what we did together and we had a lot of guys on that team in those years who were Christians. Having that bond made our relationship more powerful. And that faith gave me great confidence.

Jeff reminded me recently of one time when we were in Dunedin, Florida, during spring training to face the Toronto Blue Jays, and I was on the trip to get in an inning of work. There were several young pitchers who would go on the bus rides. We all were sitting in the bullpen waiting to pitch, and all these guys were asking me questions. One of the young pitchers asked me if I ever got nervous when I was pitching, and I said that I felt very calm, that I felt like I was born to do this, that I don't ever get nervous. I was under control. Whenever we were in spring training, I was surrounded by all those young pitchers, and they always were asking me those type of questions.

Man, I didn't get nervous. That was part of doing my job, and you do your best to do it well. I didn't ever think about the outcome— good or bad. I always tell people: I know who I trust and I know who I am. With that I know the Lord gave me the strength, and He gave me the tools for me to be successful. So I always mentioned that to the younger pitchers. Many of them were Hispanic, and they knew what I meant when I was saying that.

We already had won a World Series in 1996 before Jeff got there, but we won three championships in a row in his first three seasons, beginning in 1998. Jeff contributed in a mighty way. He was one of the people responsible for us staying healthy and fit from the beginning of spring training in February through the World Series in late October. To keep everyone ready for such a long season was not easy. Winning the World Series in '98 in his first year was amazing, but he had the responsibility to keep guys in shape and hungry those next couple of years, too, and he did that well. I appreciated every push that he gave me, every motivational talk to stay on course to win those championships. That doesn't just come along. You not only need to have a group of individuals on the field who have the talent and the hunger to win, but also a manager like Joe Torre and the coaches and the trainers.

A lot of teams have won it all once, but not a lot of teams have won three championships in a row or four out of five years like we did from 1996 to 2000. It's all about staying hungry.

I always appreciated Jeff having such a big role on the team, but sometimes people took it for granted. People see what we do on the field, but there are so many people behind us and behind the scenes who were helping. Jeff was one of the people who was pushing us. That's what you need from a coach. You need him to be right on top of you, telling you that you have to do this for the team to be successful. Jeff was one of those people for us and especially for me.

Jeff would always say that he didn't need to recreate the wheel with me, that I was like a racehorse that he had to just get warmed up. After that he'd just let me roll. God gifted me with the physical tools and the psychological makeup and confidence, but we all need a push sometimes, and Jeff definitely did that for me. It wasn't ever a problem or hard for me because that's what I wanted. I wanted to be the best and he always kept me and our team right on track for that. I wasn't lazy by any means, but sometimes we all need a push to pay attention to all those little things.

Jeff was no longer with the team by the time I injured my knee in Kansas City in 2012, when I tore my ACL doing something I loved to do: shagging those fly balls in batting practice. I knew right away that, even though I was 42 years old, I could not retire on that injury. I had to come back and pitch again. The last thing I wanted people to remember about me was me laying on the warning track at Kauffman Stadium. I feel blessed that I was able to come back the following year for one final season, adding the final 44 saves of my all-time record 652 that I recorded with the Yankees.

While I was doing the rehab from my surgery, even though I did not have Jeff with me at that time, I always recalled the things that we talked about. It was crazy. I had someone else pushing me to the max so I could make it back, but I never forgot the things Jeff and I used to discuss and how he pushed me. I was turning 43 and I didn't have anything to prove to anyone if I retired right then. But my heart and my commitment to the Yankees and to the game allowed me to make that comeback. It happened only because of the grace of God and the coaches pushing me day in and day out, but that rehab for me also symbolized my relationship with Jeff and what he did for me all those years we were together.

I had worked with him for so many years that the work ethic and that mentality was in me. I didn't have to be reminded of the work that I needed to do in my rehab. Jeff put that in my brain, and I had my routine of every day doing what I needed to do. I knew everything would turn out right. That was the type of person that Jeff was for me and my career. I never will forget what he did for me and our time together.

—**Mariano Rivera** *played all 19 of his seasons in Major League Baseball with the New York Yankees. He is MLB's all-time leader in saves (652) and the only player in baseball history to be unanimously elected to the Baseball Hall of Fame in Cooperstown, New York.*

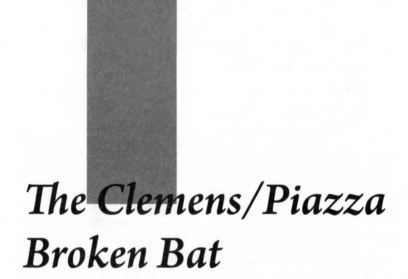

The Clemens/Piazza
Broken Bat

ONE OF THE MOST SIGNIFICANT AND CONTROVERSIAL PIECES OF New York baseball memorabilia of at least the past half-century was just sitting there, waiting to be discarded. I feel like so much of my professional life over more than three decades in Major League Baseball—two separate stints with the New York Yankees wrapped around one with the rival New York Mets—has been beholden to the mantra "right place, right time." This was the perfect example.

The jagged bat shard that Yankees pitcher Roger Clemens caught and then infamously hurled in the direction of Mets catcher Mike Piazza in Game 2 of the 2000 World Series tangibly symbolized the oddball blood feud between two of baseball's and New York's biggest stars at the time. Yes, I wanted it, so I took it. And I later sold it.

In his first career appearances against the seven-time Cy Young winner as a member of the Mets, Piazza had gone deep against Clemens in two separate games in the summer of 1999 and then added a grand slam against "The Rocket" in June 2000. Less than one month later, Piazza was beaned in the helmet by a Clemens fastball in the second game of a doubleheader, giving him a concussion and forcing him out of that year's All-Star Game.

So there already was some unmistakable friction hanging over the situation on October 23 when Clemens took the ball in Game 2 of the Fall Classic, the first between two New York teams since the

Yankees had faced the Brooklyn Dodgers in 1956, one year before their departure for Los Angeles. The Yankees already had taken the opener in dramatic fashion—4–3 in 12 innings—but everything was unquestionably heightened the next night as the drama built between Clemens and Piazza. Everyone was wondering: is Clemens going to come inside at all? Are they going to let bygones be bygones and just try to get this guy out, or is he going to try to send another message? It didn't take long to find out.

The very first inning, Clemens recorded two quick outs, and the count was 1–2 when Piazza got sawed off. What happened next was one of the most bizarre, yet unforgettable, October sports moments that people have talked about ever since. The bat shattered in three pieces. Piazza had the little handle still in his hands. One piece went flying toward the Mets' dugout on the third-base side, and one piece (the barrel) bounded directly to Clemens, who inexplicably chucked it past Piazza toward our dugout.

I truly don't know what Roger was thinking—I know he said he thought the barrel of the bat was actually the ball—but I do know that he used to get so wound up, so amped to pitch. So I thought it was kind of a cross between maybe trying to put some more fear into Piazza, or that he was disgruntled about the bat coming at him and just lost his wits and was like "to hell with that thing."

So he fired it in Piazza's direction, and when he did, it bounced a couple of times, and then the sharp end of the barrel just stuck in the ground right near our on-deck circle. Of course, the benches cleared, but when the confrontation finally got settled down a little bit, Clemens was just standing there waiting for another ball. There are pictures of it where Piazza is just kind of staring back at Clemens like *What the hell?*

In all the commotion, unbeknownst to anybody, one of our batboys ran out and did what they would do all the time, which is collect the pieces of the shattered bat and bring them back into our dugout to throw them away. Usually no one thinks twice about it, but I noticed this bat was just sitting there in the corner near the bat rack and up against the cement wall in the corner, where I stood quite often during games, just above the stairwell that led into the dugout.

After things calmed down and the third out of the inning was recorded, everybody was just kind of going about their business between innings. All I kept thinking was this bat is just going to be discarded, and at the time, I thought to myself, *I'm going to grab this thing.*

Right at the end of the inning after the Mets were retired, the organist was playing during the three-minute break. Nobody said a word to me. Nobody ever mentioned to me that they saw me grab the bat. I guess no one even noticed. If they did, fine. They could have approached me, but I just bent down and grabbed it and walked up the ramp to the clubhouse and put in my locker between innings. The game went on, and afterward I simply took it home with me. I had it until 2014. So we're talking 14 years of owning a true piece of baseball history. No one ever knew I had it. And nobody ever asked the group, "Hey, did anyone take Piazza's broken bat?"

When I put it back in my locker, there was this little cubby at the bottom where you could lift up the lid, so I put it in there. When I left that night, I had a duffel bag that I was taking home with some clothes in there, and again no one said a word to me about anything. It ended up being displayed in my office at my home for years. I had it on a shelf along with some photo clippings of the incident and a *Sports Illustrated* picture of Clemens in the midst of throwing the barrel of the bat.

Only a few good friends of mine knew about it. No one affiliated with the Yankees realized it. Besides my family I would probably say no more than five or 10 people knew I had it. It wasn't like I was saying, "Wow, you've got to come see this." But those people always would remark that it was such a big piece of New York baseball history and memorabilia. In passing over the years, I thought I should get Clemens and Piazza to sign it, but I always decided against it. What if they wanted it? So I just let it go and kept it as a keepsake for years.

But then came 2014, eight years after I was let go by the Yankees for a second time. I thought that I'd had it long enough. I made a few calls, did some research, and came across Heritage Auctions out of Dallas. They're a big auction house, so I called them and told them, "I may have a rare piece of memorabilia that might interest you folks."

At first, they were real short with me, giving me the third degree, asking, "Who are you with?"

I explained to them who I was and finally I said, "Do you remember the barrel of the bat that Roger Clemens threw at Mike Piazza in the 2000 World Series?" Instantly, I could sense the attention of the young lady that I was speaking with, and her interest was rising. So I said, "Well, I have that."

They wanted to know how I acquired it, and I told them what my position was with the Yankees at the time. She put me on hold again and transferred me to someone else. I knew I had their attention now. One of their directors got on the phone, and I retold the story and informed them I was considering selling this piece. We immediately started the authentication process, and I had no problem with that. I knew it was the real deal. It was pretty easy to prove. I did my research on Piazza and knew that any bat that he used should have shoe polish and scuff marks on the top of the barrel because he always used to slam it against his cleats.

I checked out the bat, and, sure enough, there were cleat marks in addition to his name and the Mizuno brand logo that he used. Even all those years later, there also were some small traces of Yankee Stadium dirt still on the sharp end of the bat from where it had stuck into the ground. I figured that couldn't hurt the sale price.

Obviously, they also matched up pictures and videos from that night to authenticate the shape of the piece. So I had no problem waiting out that process. A few days later, I went to New York City to another one of their offices, and they securely mailed it to their facility. About a week later, they got back to me and said, "This is clean. This is definitely what you say it is."

So they set up the auction for February 22, 2014, at the Fletcher-Sinclair Mansion on the Upper East Side in Manhattan. I still have the book advertising the various items available. There were probably 30 or 40 things, including Muhammad Ali's boxing gloves, Joe Frazier's shoes, and some Kareem Abdul-Jabbar memorabilia. The night before the auction was held, they had a dinner for us in the city, and many of the items and owners were there. So the bat was on display alongside some of the other cool things that would be auctioned off the following night. Obviously, I was excited. I was thinking, *Wow, this is really something.*

People asked me afterward if I needed clearance from the Yankees or from Piazza to sell the item, but it was in my possession, and no one ever contested it. No one ever stepped forward to dispute it, even though about a week beforehand, there were articles in various newspapers stating that the bat was going to be sold. The auction house obviously wanted to get some publicity for the collectors, stating that I was the possessor of the item. I heard nothing from anyone from the Yankees about it.

The auction started about 7:30 PM, and my possession was either Item No. 23 or No. 24. It was live-streamed, so people did not have to be there in person to bid. There were people on phones taking bids in that manner, and there were probably 50-to-60 bidders and people like myself seated in the audience. As it got closer to go time, the auctioneer explained what my item was—not that it needed much explanation to sports fans. It was up on the large viewing screen, and the descriptions and timeline were given.

Experts initially thought it would fetch about $10,000. So when it came time, my heart was racing. I would have been happy with that amount, but I had no idea how high it would go and was hoping for more. Pretty quickly I could tell it would go for significantly more. I figured there were some people waiting in the wings who were laying low on it and didn't want to have competition. So I was anxious, definitely nervous. It was something I'd never been a part of before. They didn't mention who I was or my former employment with the Yankees or anything like that.

They started off the bidding at $2,500, but then it moved up pretty quickly from there past $10,000, to $15,000, $17,500, $22,500, and so on. Before we knew it, it ultimately sold for $47,800. I was shocked. One of the thoughts in the back of my mind was that maybe Clemens would buy it. Or Piazza. Or someone who was a known collector like broadcaster Keith Olbermann, who had a weird connection to the Yankees. His mother actually was once struck in the stands behind our dugout by a wild throw from second baseman Chuck Knoblauch.

I never did find out the name of the buyer, but it ended up going for $47,800. Perhaps part of that exorbitant number was because I had mentioned in the articles leading up to the auction that a portion of the proceeds would go to the CJ Foundation for SIDS, a charity near and dear to my family's hearts after my wife Gale and I had lost our daughter Shannon to Sudden Infant Death Syndrome in 1992.

We also had to pay the auction house a percentage of the total and we made a $5,000 donation to the CJ Foundation. The remaining amount helped us with the cost of our other children's college tuitions. It was a time period where my older son had already finished college, but my other two kids were still in high school. The money definitely helped us, and it's not like I blew it on some crazy vacation or any frivolous purchases.

Over the years there was nothing else I've auctioned off from my time in baseball. I have my three World Series rings from the Yankees and I cherish them. I never was one to ask players to sign things for me because I know how much that perturbs them. I always considered myself part of the team, so I didn't ever want to be part of that at all. I do have a ton of cherished baseballs and pictures that I've received from being a member of those championship teams. There were some cool things that were signed, but those were more for me to have. I have a catcher's mitt signed by Yogi Berra, but that is the kind of stuff that I want to pass on to my children.

Even when the stories came out that I sold the Piazza bat for more than $47,000, it was surprising that not one former player, coach, front-office person, or PR person from the Yankees reached out to me to express disbelief that I had the bat in my possession for all those years. Not one person. Not even Clemens or Piazza. I always found that part of it very strange, but I really was elated by the amount of money we received for it. After the auction I drove home that night. My wife, who was down in Florida where she's from originally, was visiting her family. I gave her a call to let her know, and she was ecstatic.

Still, the lack of inquiry always seemed crazy to me. It was such a cool piece of baseball history to have at my house for so many years. To have that bat in my family's possession for that period of time was very special. I would love to know its whereabouts today. There is so much Yankees history—and memorabilia as a result. There are home-run balls hit by Babe Ruth or Roger Maris or Reggie Jackson or Derek Jeter. The Piazza bat, though, definitely stands out as a unique stand-alone item especially since it's from the lone World Series ever played between the Bronx Bombers and their crosstown rivals, the Mets.

When I think about this unforgettable moment, all of the controversy swirling around it and then the wonderment of whatever happened to the bat, it was just so cool to be a small part of that storyline playing out. It was just one of those instances when being at the right place at the right time really worked out for me.

Mr. Torre

FROM MY FIRST YEAR WITH JOE TORRE IN 1998, THE MOST ADMIRABLE aspect of his personality to me always was just how consistently calm he was, no matter the circumstance. He definitely made it a point to never show a lot of emotion in the dugout—whether things were going well or poorly. If somebody got picked off or missed a sign, he wouldn't jump on their case. More often than not, the offending player would come off the field, knowing that he fouled up and had made a mistake. At some point, usually within a minute or two, he would make his way over to Torre and to Don Zimmer and say something along the lines, "Skip, I know I messed up."

Torre wouldn't ever embarrass guys, as I'd seen other managers do in the past. Whether it was Derek Jeter or the 25th man on our roster, they always would take it upon themselves. Those teams in the dynasty years policed the clubhouse from within. Being the great player that he was, Torre always talked about how he learned as much during a season that he struggled as he did from 1971, when he won the National League MVP after batting .363 for the St. Louis Cardinals. And from all the teams that he'd managed before coming to the Yankees in 1996, he had developed a patience and an ability to trust his staff and the leaders of the team without feeling the need to micromanage every aspect of the operation.

Physically, I know that Torre liked to work out six or seven days a week. If we had a day game, he would meet me early in the morning, and if it was a night game, we would meet late in the afternoon, always at the stadium, whether we were home or on the road. I knew his time was short before games, so the time period directing him through his workout was very special to me. Torre would usually knock out 30 minutes on the StairMaster, and then I would direct him through 30 minutes of strength training. He grew fond of increasing his strength, and I aided him to understand the benefits of sport-specific strength training for baseball. I think it also might have helped with some of the anxiousness or stress. Getting his blood flowing before every game seemed to make him feel good. Whenever he'd work out, you could sense him thinking about the multiple plates he had spinning and the moves he might make to resolve those decisions.

Beginning with my first year with Torre in 1998, I also would make him a protein drink that I'd bring to him in the dugout around the second inning. The contents were vanilla protein, banana, apple juice, and ice, and it was probably around 14 to 16 ounces. He really enjoyed them, and it reached a point where pitching coach Mel Stottlemyre started drinking them, too.

We went out with Torre and the other coaches about 10 or 12 times a season, especially if we were flying into a city on an off day. If our plane landed at 6:00 PM or so, Torre would have a big dinner set up, so that trainers Gene Monahan, Steve Donohue, myself, and all the coaches would get a chance to eat at one of the best restaurants in every city. They'd all just open the doors for Torre. We called it "the Torre Meal," and it would go on for nearly three hours. Torre definitely knew his restaurants and he had a favorite spot in every city.

They were so enjoyable because of the camaraderie, the laughs, and the stories that would come out of it. One that stands out was when were in Montreal in 2000. Lee Mazzilli was on the staff then, and somebody brought up the name of Bob Gibson. Torre loved to talk about Gibson, one of his prominent former teammates with the Cardinals. Monahan told a story about running into Gibson during the offseason at an airport and he said, "That son of a gun wouldn't give me a minute of time."

Gibson was known as an ornery cuss, and Torre was sitting there listening to the story as Monahan continued spouting off about him. Torre and Gibson were the best of friends, so Torre pulled out his cell phone. Before he dialed he asked Monahan what he would say to Gibson if he was at the table right at that moment. Monahan said he'd mention that he was a fan of his but wished he treated people better. Torre then called Gibson on his cell and said, "Hey Gibby, I got a guy here who wants talk to you."

Monahan was flabbergasted. Put on the spot, Monahan grabbed the phone while everyone was dying laughing and was unfailingly polite. He said, "Hi, Mr. Gibson. Yes, Mr. Torre has the staff out for a great dinner tonight and do hope you have a nice evening, sir."

It was great. That's kind of an example of the people that Torre knows and the connections he made in six decades in the game. You knew that anything could happen. The meals not only brought about great stories, but also the best of food and wine.

Even while battling prostate cancer during spring training in 1999, he told me he wanted to continue to work out as much as he could, and while beloved bench coach Don Zimmer was running the team, Torre would come into the stadium early in the morning or early in the afternoon (if we had a night game), and we would work out together. Now and again, he would watch games from the luxury boxes. I told him if there was anything I could research or do to help him with his recovery, I would do whatever he needed.

To that end, respect was such a big part of his success with the Yankees. He would give respect to all of the players and staff, and everyone would reciprocate that back to him. You knew he might not always say anything, but he'd see everything. Handling that special group of players during the season, he would joke and say that his job was to just "not mess it up."

He was so much more important than that, of course. But that team was so good, and he relied heavily on Zim and Stottlemyre and the other coaches, guys like Willie Randolph, Jose Cardenal, Chris Chambliss, and Tony Cloninger during the championship years and later Mazzilli, Don Mattingly, and a few others. It was such a great staff because every one of them had success in the major leagues, and they understood what the players were going through. I think they also knew how great a team we had, and there was little need to try to recreate the wheel.

The Yankees won the World Series in four of Torre's first five years with the team, and I was there for three of them. Although we didn't win another championship during the remainder of his tenure, he managed the team for a dozen years altogether, and they made the playoffs every season.

Midwestern Roots

HOW DOES A SPORTS FANATIC FROM A SMALL TOWN IN IOWA WIND UP working for George Steinbrenner and winning multiple World Series rings with the fabled New York Yankees in the City That Never Sleeps? Well, my sports aspirations began in the Hawkeye State and took me through stops in big-time college football programs at Nebraska and Florida before landing in the Bronx.

I was born in 1954 in Washington, Iowa, which boasted a population of around 5,900 at the time. It's situated in the southeastern part of the state about 20 miles south of Iowa City, which is where the University of Iowa is located. By the time I was in first grade, we had relocated to Sioux City. By "we" I mean the five of us kids at the time. I have a brother Greg, who is five years older than I; twin sisters Cathy and Chris, who are four years older than I; and another sister Karen, who is one year behind them. I also have a younger brother Mark, who came 10 years later. He was the little surprise baby for our family.

My father Frank was a radio broadcaster—news, sports, you name it—though he also did some TV work. He actually was quite an important voice in our area. For a time he also was president of the Iowa Broadcasting Association. He used to do color commentary for the University of Iowa basketball games, and then what moved us to Sioux City was his new job with WNAX Radio. It was an AM station out of Yankton, South Dakota, but it had a massive reach across the Midwest. The station was known at the time to have the tallest radio tower in the United States, which had the capacity to reach up to 35 states on clear night.

Following my dad's lead, we were a big sports family. My dad was a state-record long jumper in high school in Iowa. My twin sisters played in the state finals in high school in tennis and went on to play at Iowa State. My brothers and I also played tennis with the family. Mom and Dad would take us, and they had all great strokes. Back then, probably around 1968 or '69, women's athletics weren't as big as they are now—they didn't have Title IX at that time—but my sisters were highly accomplished at the sport. I also played tennis with the family. My dad would take us, and they all had these great tennis strokes. I would use two hands like a baseball bat to hit the ball. I wasn't much of a tennis player, but I was hitting the ball a long way.

My mom Margaret graduated from Grinnell College and worked for Catholic Charities, which helped direct and organize adoptions and placements for unwed mothers. My mom had a special calm about her to console and comfort not only our family, but also others in need. My parents worked hard to support a family of six children and were proud to have all six become college graduates, which was not the norm at the time.

Sports definitely played a huge role in my childhood. I played football, basketball, and baseball from grade school through high school. I pitched and played center field and shortstop in baseball. I was a quarterback in football until moving to tight end and defensive end while attending Heelan High School in Sioux City. I also played basketball and participated in track and field for the school. If you were an athlete back then, you often played three or more sports.

Playing and following sports was a passion. When I was a young boy—probably somewhere between eight and 10 years old—I would listen to every St. Louis Cardinals baseball game at night like so many kids in that part of the country. Most of us either were Chicago Cubs fans or Cardinals fans, but some rooted for the Kansas City Royals or the Minnesota Twins because you could get all those games on the radio at night. My heroes clearly were the Cardinals. Jack Buck, Harry Caray, and later on Mike Shannon, broadcast the games. It would be a great night when the Cardinals were on the West Coast. I'd go to bed listening to the Cards playing the Los Angeles Dodgers—Bob Gibson vs. Don Drysdale or Sandy Koufax and all those guys. We had Steve Carlton when he was young. It was very exciting later in life to have the opportunity to meet many of these people as part of my career. Bill White was the first baseman. Tim McCarver was the catcher. Man, they had some great teams. Lou Brock, Curt Flood, and Orlando Cepeda also were heroes of mine. KMOX out of St. Louis had this tremendous reach across the U.S, and I, too, took advantage of it.

Back then they still had scheduled doubleheaders on Sundays, and three summers in a row, my dad, my older brother Greg, and I drove from Sioux City to Chicago. While en route we'd spend Sunday nights in Washington, Iowa, where I was born. We'd stay at my Aunt Sally's house. And from there on Sunday mornings, we'd drive the final 250 miles to Chicago to watch the Cubs play against the Cardinals in doubleheaders. We were on the third-base side in Wrigley Field all the way up. I had to be no more than 10 or 11, but I saw Gibson pitch in person. I remember Larry Jaster and Dick Hughes, too. I never got to St. Louis for a game, but Wrigley was just incredible, and seeing players like Ernie Banks, Ron Santo, Billy Williams was amazing.

From Sioux City to Chicago is probably nine hours in the car, so that's why we'd split up the ride. Later on, I also saw a couple of Major League Baseball games at Comiskey Park, the home of the

Chicago White Sox. My mom actually was a huge Ted Williams fan, and we road tripped to Comiskey to see him and the Boston Red Sox. When I was really young, maybe five or six, I came down with scarlatina, a form of scarlet fever. My parents were hellbent to go see Ted Williams play. I vaguely remember sitting down the left-field foul line just so my mom could see The Splendid Splinter. Just like the rest of the family, Mom was a massive sports fan. I remember my dad had to carry me into the game at the old Comiskey Park because I was too weak to walk and had a blanket wrapped around me, but hey, we saw Teddy Ballgame.

As a sports reporter, my father recorded quite a few high-profile, one-on-one interviews. Some of his work should be in Cooperstown at the Baseball Hall of Fame. One example is an interview he did with baseball legend Rogers Hornsby. Dad even had in his possession for several years a game-worn shirt from Babe Ruth with his name stitched on it and an autographed baseball from The Bambino. Yankees minority owner and noted memorabilia collector Barry Halper purchased both items from him for $20,000.

My father passed away during my second stint with the Yankees in 2001, and I'll never forget how thoughtful the organization was during this grieving period. It's actually quite a story. We were coming back from the All-Star break in July and had just resumed the second half of the season. We were in Miami playing the Florida Marlins. At that time my Mom also had suffered a massive stroke and she was living in an assisted living facility in Sioux City. The stroke had intensified to the point that she had lost her ability to speak and the use of her right side.

My dad was still living at home and he'd go up to Holy Spirit Retirement Home to visit my mom every day. As a family, we decided to make an effort to have Dad move there into an active living facility and be close to Mom. We also had spoken with a priest about utilizing the independent living section of the retirement home for this purpose. He was very obstinate. An independent guy, he wanted no part of that. Finally, he agreed to a meeting at the same retirement home. My brothers and sisters were coming back into town and they were going to meet with Dad, the director of the facility, and a priest to see about getting him to utilize the independent living section of the retirement home. My siblings told me about the meeting, and I was going to phone in to participate at 8:00 PM that night from Florida. Our game started around 7:15, and I told Joe Torre, "Listen, about 8:00, I've got an important family phone call to make." I told him what it was about and that I wouldn't be on the bench for about a half an hour or so.

After stretching the team, I went into the clubhouse and used the visiting clubhouse manager's office to call into the meeting. Somebody in the family answered the phone. I think it was my sister Chris. All my Mom could do was kind of mutter. She had her faculties and understanding, but she couldn't talk. And then I said, "Hello, Dad. How's everybody doing?"

And then all of a sudden all I heard was: "Oh my God! Oh no!" I'm thinking, *Whoa, what's going on here?*

My dad had a massive heart attack. That's how I found out. Here I am in the clubhouse in Florida and wondering what the hell is going on. And my sister got on and said, "Jeff, Dad just had a heart attack or something. We'll call you right back."

He had fallen right to the floor from the meeting table. So I hung up the phone, and I'm freaking out and waiting for them to call me back. I went back to my locker for a minute, and Roger Clemens was the only person in there. His locker was either right next to mine or two lockers down. He was leaving and was getting dressed. I believe he was going to pitch the next day in the next city. Clemens said, "What are you doing in here? What's going on?"

I said, "I was just on the phone with my family. I think my dad just died." He was the first person that I told.

About a half-hour later, I made contact back with my family, and they told me that he had in fact passed away. My wife and my son Sean were back at the hotel in Miami. They were down there for the All-Star break, and we had spent a few days together over the break. So I contacted them, and we met back at the hotel and made plans to get back to Iowa. Whenever I think of that stadium down there in Florida, I don't have good memories of it. We also lost Games 4 and 5 of the 2003 World Series there to the Marlins before they clinched in the next game in the Bronx, but this was not a good place for me for deeper, more personal reasons.

My father had attended St. Ambrose College (now a university), a small NAIA school located in Davenport, Iowa, about 120 miles outside Chicago. That's where I went too. The enrollment at the time probably was about 1,200 to 1,400 students for the entire school. I didn't really consider going to a bigger school such as Iowa or Iowa State because I wanted to be able to play baseball. I came close to committing to play football at Dakota State, another small school in South Dakota, with another friend from high school. But my father having attended St. Ambrose was another big selling point.

I played two years of baseball there and then switched and did two years of track and field. I threw the shotput and the discus, which I'd also done in high school. Back in the early '70s in Iowa, the baseball season didn't start usually until school was out. The track season would end in late May or early June, and then I'd play the baseball season. At the onset of college, I was considering becoming a coach and a physical education teacher. By the last semester of junior year, I started doing some practical work in the field. I did some hands-on substitute teaching and assisted physical education classes in local schools.

I quickly found out this was not for me. I wasn't sure I had the patience to deal with some of these young kids. I had a sports background and thought perhaps I could do something sports-related such as get into the business side of it to be a sales rep for Adidas or Rawlings. I initially stayed in Davenport upon graduation in 1977 and worked for the United Parcel Service. I began working for UPS my senior year. I was at the facility there from 4:30 until 7:30 AM. After graduation I stayed on and delivered packages during the peak season during Christmas. That lasted until 1978, but that spring I moved in with Cathy and her family in Lincoln, Nebraska.

She knew of a sporting goods store there called Lawlor's and told me I could get a job there. She also said I could live with her for a while until I got on my feet. I ended up doing that.

I worked the floor, sold shoes, worked the cash register, etc. Again, however, I quickly found out this line of work was not for me either. I didn't enjoy that at all. I worked there for about four months.

During fall Saturdays, especially when the University of Nebraska had a home football game, there was absolutely nothing else going on in town. The store was open, but all you could hear were the occasional roars of the crowd, even though the stadium was blocks away. It was always a massive crowd. When Missouri came to town to play Nebraska, Phil Bradley was the quarterback. Kellen Winslow was the tight end, and James Wilder was the running back. That talented Missouri team came to Lincoln and beat Nebraska. Years later, I always had a very good relationship with Bradley, who mostly played with the Seattle Mariners in his eight seasons in the majors and then went on to be a representative for the Players' Association. Whenever I saw him, we'd always strike up a conversation about the Missouri–Nebraska games.

About two blocks away from the sporting goods store was the local YMCA. I had always enjoyed working out, lifting weights, and trying to increase my strength. I knew early on that it was important to try to optimize performance. I also liked to be in good shape and to feel strong. When I was at the YMCA one day, a professor from the University of Nebraska was there, and we struck up a conversation. He had commented that I worked out pretty hard—beyond what the normal individual does at the YMCA.

It was Dr. Keith Pritchard. He was friends with Boyd Epley, who was the head strength and conditioning coach for the Cornhuskers football team and the entire sports program. The legendary Epley is known as the godfather of implementing and optimizing performance through strength training and conditioning exercises in sports-specific regimens that became synonymous with Nebraska. He was the first true strength and conditioning coach in college football.

Dr. Pritchard contacted Epley and arranged for my interview with him. Incredibly, I soon became a volunteer assistant with the football program under coach Tom Osborne. My days at the sporting goods store were over, and I started a three-decade-long strength training career.

People usually are being facetious when they say they'd do a job for nothing, but I never was paid in my three seasons as a volunteer assistant with the strength and conditioning program at Nebraska. The non-compensatory experience still could not have been more valuable to my career. It was more about the opportunity to work and learn inside the pioneering weight training program Epley began in 1969, which launched the careers of dozens of former assistants to collegiate and professional teams across the United States.

I no longer worked regular shifts at Lawlor's, instead tailoring my weekly schedule with odd jobs that fit in with my new hours doing anything asked of me by Epley and Coach Osborne with the Cornhuskers. Mike Arthur also has been Epley's top assistant since

1976, and Arthur took me under his wing and became a mentor. Arthur often would have the first crack at jobs with teams that contacted Epley, but he never left. Arthur's research into optimal athletic performance via strength and conditioning is a prime reason for Nebraska's on-field success.

What I would do mostly was work as a substitute teacher some mornings and early afternoons in the local public school systems. It would be high school one day, middle school or grade schools on others. Beyond the teaching I also occasionally drove a construction truck, hauling asphalt and dirt, just trying to make ends meet. I would finish around 2:00 PM or so and I'd go right from there to the university weight room, where I would just follow the day's activities of whatever needed to get done. Epley knew I was working construction and hauling dirt to various sites and said he would appreciate it if I ever had a chance to bring some dirt to his backyard. I obviously wanted to please the boss, so I took a chance and deviated from the scheduled driving route and headed to Epley's house and dumped a full load of dirt. He was so thrilled with me doing this that I did it one more time. Those two truckloads of dirt saved him some money and scored major brownie points for me.

My first football-related responsibility at Nebraska was painting the weights, which was not the most exciting job, to say the least. It actually turned into a competitive thing because there were so many of us in the same position, and we considered all of the different tasks on the bottom rung to be a competition.

Eventually, I worked my way up to Epley's top assistant, and other schools started calling him about me. Occasionally they were professional teams, but mostly collegiate teams would call him. It was recognized that we worked our way up to what became known as the launching pad. That's what we called it. For example, Gary Wade, the gentleman who left before me, went to the Detroit

Lions and from there he went to Clemson and is still part of Dabo
Swinney's great program. Steve Schultz was another guy who left
before Wade and went to Stanford. Probably eight or 10 assistants of
Epley's went all around the country. Jerry Schmidt at Oklahoma was
another one. All these of major powerhouses were contacting Epley
and asking, "Hey, do you have somebody who could help direct our
program?"

Nebraska was really the pioneer in this field. The crazy thing is
none of us even got paid when we were there. I know that I never did.
I was there for two-and-a-half years, but it was such a great learning
experience and really opened my eyes toward major college athletics
and the feeling of gameday and large crowds. We didn't get to travel
with the team as volunteer assistants, but we got to be right there on
the sidelines in Lincoln, even though that almost ended on the first
day for me.

We were playing against Penn State on Saturday, and on
Friday afternoons, the visiting teams would come to town and do a
walkthrough in our stadium. Penn State–Nebraska was the Game of
the Week on ABC and being announced by the great Keith Jackson.
I saw the Nittany Lions come out and walk the field before they
went in and got dressed. They all had on these blue blazers and
turtlenecks and dress pants and were led by Joe Paterno.

I was on the sideline prior to the kickoff of the game, and a wire
fence separated the field from the fans. One of the fans starting
screaming, "Hey, I dropped my jersey over here. Can you pick that
up for me?" I looked over, and there was this red mesh thing, which
looked like a jersey, laying on our side of the fence on our sideline.
I went over and picked it up and just handed it to the guy. It ended
up that it was the ball bag that holds about eight or 10 footballs for
the kickers and the punters. I had mistakenly given it away to one

of the fans. I got called in and aired out. I figured I was done, but fortunately they kept me around.

Since we were just lowly volunteers, we didn't travel. But just to be on the sidelines and associated with that team at that time was incredible. Nebraska had some great players like Dave Rimington, Jarvis Redwine, I.M. Hipp, Junior Miller, and Mike Rozier. Back in those days, true freshmen were not allowed to play on the varsity. I was in the press box and saw a bunch of talented freshmen on the field that day, including Turner Gill at quarterback, Irving Fryar at wide receiver, and Rozier at running back. They were putting on a show. These guys were unbelievable. We could tell the future was bright.

Rival Oklahoma led by head coach Barry Switzer and running back Billy Sims came to Lincoln when I was there. Sims ran for more than 200 yards against Nebraska. We were big and strong but slow, and Oklahoma was not as big, but the Sooners were fast, elusive, and athletic. It made Nebraska somewhat change their ways toward recruiting and training.

What set Nebraska apart at that time was our ability to test, evaluate, exercise, set goals, and then retest. So you'd really get some great information in our database. That's why Nebraska was considered at the forefront of that strength training movement. I also loved to learn about technique and the correct movements of the exercises. I learned from the best. Epley and Arthur were sticklers about doing things correctly. They were also great at motivating players. We would see the players carry that confidence to the field and have it translate into success.

Of course, like with any big-time program at the time, there also were rumors of guys doing steroids and things like that. Dean Steinkuhler was our All-American offensive guard. He was an underclassman while I was at Nebraska. I know he later admitted to using performance-enhancing drugs after he left school, but I was surprised. There was something going on, I believe that. The same thing happened with notable linemen at other schools like Bill Fralic and then Tony Mandarich. That was kind of the signal that there was a big problem because anabolic steroids were being made accessible to these young athletes.

By the end of the 1980 season, the University of Florida called about me, even though there was no personal connection there. I simply was the next one up. The Gators were the next program to call Boyd, and I was the next in line on the launching pad. When Boyd informed me of their interest, I said, "Sure, I'll interview!"

I flew into Gainesville, Florida, when Charley Pell was the football coach at Florida. Previously, he'd been at Clemson, and the Gators went 0–10–1 in 1979. The head strength and conditioning coach at Florida was Rich Tuten. A former All-American nose guard at Clemson, he'd played for Pell there. This guy was a specimen. He was about 6'1" and 265 to 270 pounds. You didn't want to mess with this guy. He was a rock. Tuten had been hired as the head strength and conditioning coach, and they wanted to bring in a full-time assistant to help the team get to the next level. Tuten and I hit it off right away and got along well. I immediately fell in love with the campus and the facilities and the opportunity. Plus, I was going to get paid. I felt like I needed a steadier job as I hit my mid-20s. I flew back to Lincoln and was gone within a week. I had about six cardboard boxes of clothes, pots, and pans. After saying good-bye to my friends and family, I headed to Florida.

I realized early on there was some major work to do. We had a meeting with the entire football coaching staff, and it came time for the strength and conditioning staff to speak. During my first few weeks there, I'd noticed that all throughout the weight room that there was something known as "the 400-pound bench press club."

That was quite a mark to bench 400 pounds. There were probably about 10 to 15 names that were up on the wall.

Still, the form and the technique used by the players benching 400 was way off. They just weren't doing it correctly. And it was showing on the field. These guys were either bouncing the bar off their chest, or some of the coaches would sort of pull the bar up so they could supposedly do the rep, but it was all false security. I knew if these players benched with correct form, that they'd bench 320 instead of 400. That's why they were getting whipped on the field. So in this meeting, I spoke up. I said, "Coach Pell, everybody, it's a mess what's going on in the weight room. It's just false security and falsity of trying to build the ego of these players. This has got to be done correctly."

One of the defensive coaches was screaming at me because two of his top players were in that 400-pound club, but I just knew that if these guys wanted to win and get stronger, they had to do it right. Coach Pell implemented a rule that the graduating seniors could continue on with that old way, but anybody else—all the incoming freshmen and other players—were going to do it the correct way. He didn't say "the Mangold Way," but it was about doing it properly to get stronger on the field. I felt good about that because what I was seeing was ridiculous.

I was at Florida through 1983. After seeing that incoming class of freshmen my first year, I got on the phone and called Arthur and my buddies at Nebraska and said, "The University of Florida is going to be a powerhouse very soon. These athletes down here are incredible." Those athletes included Neal Anderson, Wilber Marshall, Lomas Brown, and John L. Williams, who all went on to lengthy NFL careers. That immediately made the job more fun.

Shortly after I got to Florida, I also finally had my own apartment. The first few months I lived in the athletic dorm, but soon I got a place of my own. I also was able to buy a car. Eventually, after I worked in the weight room all week, the coaching staff started using me as an advance scout on the weekends, too. I would leave after practice on Friday afternoons and fly to the game of the following week's opponent. I missed being on the sidelines for Florida games, but I also really enjoyed the scouting aspect of it. The main focus was to get the game tape back to Gainesville as soon as possible. Back then it was all reel-to-reel tape, and I had to get that footage back to Gainesville by Sunday morning at the latest. I'd go upstairs to the coaches' office, and those guys were already there, drinking coffee and eating donuts. They wanted to move on right away to break down the film and get started on the next week's gameplan.

On those road assignments, I would sit up in the press box and try to uncover different nuances of the game. Before the game I'd go down close to the field and check the cadence of the quarterback to see if I could decipher their snap counts a little bit or watch the snap of the center to the holder on extra points or field-goal attempts. I was just looking for any little thing that I could pick up that might give us an advantage.

While at an Auburn game, I spoke with the father of Bo Jackson, the Heisman Trophy-winning running back who starred in both the NFL and Major League Baseball. That was very cool. He was a massive man. He had a "Jackson 34" jersey on, so I went up to him and introduced myself, thinking this had to be Bo's father, and sure enough it was. His hand went like halfway up my forearm.

My very first scouting trip was to LSU. On Sunday morning I headed through the fog to the Baton Rouge airport. I was about halfway there before realizing I didn't have the game tape. I must have left it at the hotel lobby. So I drove right across the median and basically hydroplaned on the wet road. I knew I had to get back to the hotel as fast as possible and get this tape. I drove into the parking lot, screeched in there, ran in to the hotel, and thankfully the tape still was sitting on the counter. I grabbed it and then started racing back to the airport. I got there just in time. After I returned the car, I sprinted in, but fortunately the fog had delayed most of the flights. I made the flight, but then I remember panting and catching my breath while sitting in the waiting area. Then I saw former Green Bay Packers star Paul Hornung. He must have done the LSU game on radio or TV the night before. I didn't say anything to him. He just sitting there with his legs crossed, reading the newspaper.

While I worked at Florida, I met two really important people in my life. The first was my future wife, Gale. I met her probably within the first two weeks that I was there. She was an academic advisor for the women's athletic program with the Gators. At that time the employees and the professors also had access to use our weight room. It was kind of a mess, but that's where I met her. She came in the weight room. I went right up to her and asked her out for a date. That's what got us going. The other person, who came into my life at that time, was George Steinbrenner. Meeting the two of them while I worked for Florida changed my life in every imaginable way. It certainly would never be the same.

Meeting The Boss

I DIDN'T ACTUALLY MEET GEORGE STEINBRENNER UNTIL AFTER I WAS hired by the New York Yankees, which was just before the start of spring training in 1984. The Boss, however, definitely was the reason I even was considered for the life-altering opportunity. Steinbrenner was a major booster and donated a lot of money to the University of Florida sports program. A few years later at one of the Yankees' spring trainings, he was even sitting in the stands signing autographs while wearing a Gators cap.

His company was based in Tampa and also Ocala, Florida— just south of Gainesville, where his horse farm was. I believe he thought that the rising University of Florida sports program might have someone it could recommend for a similar position with the Yankees. I don't know exactly who his main contact was there, but Bill Carr was the athletic director. There could have been some other boosters or buddies, too. Steinbrenner always ran in the circles with the big shots. And those people liked to try to run in circles with him. That was the likeliest connection.

Carr first contacted me about the Yankees' opening. Word quickly got around that the Yankees were looking for a full-time strength and conditioning coach. Our head strength coach at the time, Rich Tuten, actually declined the interview before I was considered for it. I think he was the type of guy that didn't have the patience for working with that type of professional athlete. He was very intense and he would not have the patience with the physically slighter statures and passive attitudes of a baseball player. I also think he always had his eye on the NFL, and he did end up landing a job with the Denver Broncos about a decade later.

Mike Shanahan was the offensive coordinator for two years during the time period when I was at Florida, and Shanny never looked back after making the jump to the NFL when he was hired by the Denver Broncos as wide receivers coach in 1984. In the ensuing decade, Shanahan served as head coach of the Los Angeles Raiders for two seasons (1988–89) and then returned to Denver as head coach in 1995, one year after winning a Super Bowl title with the San Francisco 49ers as their offensive coordinator. Tuten was hired by the Broncos as their head strength and conditioning coach and remained in Denver for 17 seasons, winning a couple of Super Bowl rings at the same time I was winning a few World Series titles with the Yankees.

That leads me back to my initial interview process. In mid-January I flew into LaGuardia Airport and grabbed a Bronx-bound cab ride to Yankee Stadium. I'd never even been to New York before. I had no idea that I was dropped off by the cab driver in the wrong place, near the back of the old Yankee Stadium by the trains underneath the subway trestles. I was trying frantically to find a door to get inside and I ended up walking three-quarters of the way around the stadium. I went the wrong way at first. All I saw was a couple of those metal garbage canisters with wood and cardboard inside being burned by people somewhat down on their luck who were hoping to stay warm and asking for money. With my Florida Gators travel bag across my shoulder, I was like, *Wow, okay, this is New York.* I finally found the entrance for the administrative area, which was across from the old players' parking lot.

My contact person with the Yankees was Bill Bergesch, who was the outgoing general manager, but at the time, he was in the process of being replaced by Murray Cook. Bergesch soon would move on to become GM of the Cincinnati Reds. The Yankees used to rotate those guys under Steinbrenner all the time, especially during the 1980s. (There would be five GMs, in fact, in as many years during my first stint with the team from 1984 to 1988.)

Bergesch told me that initiating a strength and conditioning program with the Yankees could be my icebreaker into Major League Baseball. He said Steinbrenner really wanted to have an aspiring young guy come in and take control and start a strength training program. "Of all the guys we've talked to, you're the guy we want," Bergesch told me.

I was offered the position right away and needed to make a quick decision. Spring training camp was to begin within a month, and I realized I could not let this opportunity pass, but I had one more important matter to figure out prior to leaving Florida. It was time for Gale and I to either get married or split up. (Hint: we are still married nearly four decades later.)

I first met Steinbrenner in a group staff meeting soon after I arrived at my first spring training camp in Fort Lauderdale, Florida. He pulled me aside early on during camp. It was right toward the end of a practice. I was walking down the right-field foul line at the stadium there, and it was really hot outside. I was getting ready for conditioning work with the players, to run them hard, to show them I meant business. "Hey, Mangold, come here a second," Steinbrenner said, waving me over. "I'll tell you what: don't give these guys too much water. Don't give them that much water at all, just keep working them."

Sure, I was taken aback. Even earlier that day, I had been on the infield, kind of preparing myself to head over to where Steinbrenner intercepted me. Jeff Torborg, who was one of the coaches at the time, asked me if I needed any help or assistance. "Don't be afraid to ask me anything," Torborg told me. "I'm sure you probably feel some eyes on you right now."

"What do you mean?" I said. "I feel fine."

"I think George is over there right now with binoculars, checking us out," Torborg said. "His eyes are on you right now, so do your thing."

I was slowly getting indoctrinated to the eyes in the sky and being checked out by The Boss.

The first day of camp, manager Yogi Berra came out to the field to introduce me to the team, as we lined up for stretching drills. I messed up my first encounter with Yogi. Because for me coming from a football background, it was always "Coach this, Coach that." That was just the terminology. I'd never used "Hey, Skip," or that lingo yet. I said "Coach, I'm Jeff Mangold, glad to meet you."

And in that deep Yogi voice, he said, "Oh, so I'm a Coach now?" That flustered me a little bit, and it told me that I needed to learn the ropes and get myself indoctrinated as soon as possible. Of course, that was Yogi's first year back as manager, too. He had been fired after one season in 1964 after retiring as a player the previous year, but that was his first year managing under Steinbrenner.

Like anyone who was in his employ during his nearly 40 years as principal owner—from the front office to the manager to the players all the way down the ticket takers and food vendors —I have a few personal go-to Steinbrenner experiences I always love to share. Barely a few games into my first Grapefruit League slate with the team, Steinbrenner already was pissed that we were getting beaten in spring training. He was getting all over Yogi, saying things like "Come on, we've got to win these games, dang it." The language might have been a bit saltier than that.

This also was the first time I witnessed firsthand Steinbrenner's infamous paranoia that someone was leaking things to the press. He even ordered me to go outside the trailer, where we held meetings, to look and see if anyone was around, just to make sure nobody was listening to our conversations. "I want you to look under the trailer, too," he told me.

I thought to myself, *This guy has got to be kidding me.* But he was The Boss and he was giving me a directive. I knew I'd better follow through on whatever he requested. I walked down the stairwell the three steps to the parking lot, following Steinbrenner's orders. Yes, I got down on my hands and knees and looked around underneath the trailer. I went back inside and said, "George, we're clear, good to go. Nobody's around. Nobody's snooping."

Not every meeting was like this, of course, but you definitely always had to be on your toes with Steinbrenner and prepared for anything. Usually in the meetings, each department would get a chance to give our updates. Head trainer Gene Monahan, for instance, would talk about some of the players who might have been a little bit banged-up, what their status was for practice, or how they were coming along. When I got my first chance to speak up, I wanted to lay out my goals for the camp, especially those first few days, and explain what I was trying to implement: a daily continuation of having the practice of stretching as a team because that had never been done before by the Yankees in such a communal fashion. It's obviously become commonplace now for the last 30 years. But previously the guys just came out and ran around a little bit and stretched some on their own. To do it in an organized and structured way, that was the first big phase that I wanted to get done.

There were stories from a couple of years prior when they tried to bring in a track coach to work with outfielder Dave Collins, their big free-agent signing from the Reds. He was a speed guy, and they thought he was going to be this big base stealer. Steinbrenner brought in a track coach, and I remember hearing all of these stories about them buying Collins and other players these cheesy track suits like aerodynamic track outfits for training.

My plan wasn't anything that wacky at least. On the very first day of spring training, Yogi came out in front of everyone, and I told everyone to line up. "For those of you who haven't met me yet, I'm Jeff Mangold. I'm the new strength and conditioning coach," I announced. "And this is what we're going to do as a series of exercises and warm-up drills and stretching drills that we're going to do every day."

I just laid things on the line right from the get-go. I'd learned that athletes usually wanted to be told what to do, especially if it was going to benefit them. They want to know the groundwork and the framework up front rather than be told halfway through or 20 games into the season to try to initiate something. I think players respected that. Still, I quickly learned that leading the daily stretch wouldn't be my only duty while working for Steinbrenner.

Pretty soon after the regular season started, Steinbrenner noticed that a lot of players were retreating back to the clubhouse rather than staying in the dugout watching the end of the games. The Boss got word to me that he wanted me to stand outside the clubhouse door during games and inform the players that he didn't want them in the clubhouse. No, really, he had me standing guard and refusing entry to the players to their clubhouse. One night Steinbrenner came bounding down the hallway around the third inning to check and see if I indeed wasn't letting anybody inside.

As if this story wasn't wild enough, we were standing together talking when we looked down the runway to the dugout and saw Yogi was on the phone. But we also could plainly see that the cord was ripped out, just dangling beneath the handset, and Yogi didn't realize immediately that there was no connection. I was later told that Lou Piniella had been pissed off the inning before and tore the cord out of the wall. Anyway, Yogi's got the no-longer-functioning phone to his ear, trying to get one of the relievers up for the next inning, and the phone cord was just hanging there. Steinbrenner looked at me as if to say, *What the hell is this?* He didn't storm down the runway and say anything, though I'm sure he said something afterward, but he clearly was flustered and angered by what he just saw.

I had three rotating managers in my five seasons during that first stint with the Yankees: Yogi, Billy Martin, and Piniella, though there were five managerial changes during that period.

In the 1980s, especially, you had to always be on your toes. There were so many changes, so many managers, coaches, GMs, so many moving parts. Steinbrenner definitely was more in play during the '80s than he was when I returned to the team in 1998. The '80s were his absolute craziest. That was his heyday. In the '70s they'd won a couple of championships in 1977–78. And he was still relatively new as owner, even though he had his clashes with Reggie Jackson and Martin and others. In the '80s he was always signing these different free agents and impulsively trading away prospects and changing managers and GMs like other people change their socks. He wouldn't really delegate authority. He was the only authority. In the '70s he signed big names like Jackson and Catfish Hunter and some others, but once the '80s hit, it just became a free-for-all because the winning stopped. That's what Steinbrenner was all about. He just could not stand to lose.

It was exhilarating to be in meetings with Steinbrenner because you just didn't know what he was going to say or what was going to happen. He's the type of person that you just can't take your eyes off. When he's around, he's a spectacle. He was a dapper dresser, always sharp. He noticed everything. Nothing could get by him. No detail was too small. After a practice once in Fort Lauderdale, for example, he came through the clubhouse, which was really small and tight. He walked slowly and when he got to the back of the room he turned to Pete Sheehy and Nick Priore, the longtime clubhouse attendants. "I counted only 48 chairs in here," he said. "There should be 52. There's only 48. Get more chairs in here right now."

He was definitely into the details, that's for sure. He always wanted precision. According to Peter Botte's book, *The Big 50: New York Yankees*, Steinbrenner was doing a magazine interview in his office at Yankee Stadium, and a stadium concessionaire walked in. Steinbrenner pulled out a pretzel from his drawer and complained that there wasn't enough salt on the pretzel. It's truly just like the caricature of him from *Seinfeld*. You couldn't even make up some of the things he did and said. You couldn't believe that this stuff actually happened.

Another time in spring training in either 1985 or '86, we were having another meeting in the trailer. It was early afternoon around 1:30 PM, and then all of a sudden, all hell broke loose with the weather. We were supposed to play a night game, and I'm pretty sure it was against the New York Mets. You knew Steinbrenner already was worked up about that because in those days we didn't play the Mets during the regular season. He always wanted to beat them in spring training. Then, suddenly, there were just massive amounts of rain, heavy thunderstorms, and plenty of wind, which always happens out of nowhere in Florida.

It was just me, pitching coach Mark Connor, Torborg, and a few other coaches in there with Steinbrenner. Pitching coach Sammy Ellis might have been there, too. But Steinbrenner ordered us—the coaching staff—to get out there and roll the tarp out. We were just getting drenched. The ground crew wasn't around—maybe they were at lunch or something—and the field was just going to get soaked. This was the main field, and we were out there pushing the tarp around, not even really knowing what we were doing.

Steinbrenner actually ended up getting the sheriff's department or the police department to come in with a helicopter and hover around the outfield and infield to help dry the field. It was hilarious. Steinbrenner even was out there for a while with a rake in his hand, ordering people around and telling everyone what to do to get the field ready. What can I say: he liked to get involved. In the '80s he was more physical and even more hands-on. It was beyond crazy. What's still amazing to me was that there was no ground crew there at first while Steinbrenner was directing traffic out on the field. I don't know where they were, but I'll never forget that it was us doing that work.

With Florida storms you just never know how and when they'll strike. The same also could be said about working for Tropical Storm George Steinbrenner, as I learned firsthand for much of the next two decades with a brief interruption in between. I was hired, I was fired, I was rehired and fired again just like a lot of people who worked for him. But believe me: I wouldn't trade the experience for anything.

One funny story is the time Steinbrenner gave me and a few other staffers the key to his car in Tampa and what we found inside. There was a famous Tampa steakhouse named Malio's that's not in existence anymore (they relocated), but it was right there on Dale Mabry Highway just up the road from our spring training facility. This was one of Steinbrenner's famous hangouts in Tampa.

This was after the 2002 season when we got ousted by the Anaheim Angels in the first round of the playoffs a couple of weeks after the season ended. Trainers Monahan, Steve Donohue, and myself were more or less invited—more like ordered—to fly down to Tampa for a staff meeting with Steve Swindal, Steinbrenner's then-son-in-law, and the rest of the Tampa-based crew, including team vice president

Mark Newman and several others. We flew down together, got a rental car, and went straight to Malio's. We walked in, and Monahan, who was known for his dry humor, said, "Why do I feel like I'm going to the dentist right now? We're going to get drilled here."

The hostess told us the party was waiting for us in the back room. We joined the table, and there were probably around 10 or 12 of us with our menus out, and all of a sudden, the hostess came through these saloon-style doors and said, "Mr. Steinbrenner called and said to go ahead with your meeting and your meal. He might not make it."

All of us took a deep breath, thinking Steinbrenner wasn't going to make it. Five or 10 minutes went by, and we started ordering. They even had stone crabs from Miami flown in.

Of course, just then Steinbrenner came bursting through the swinging doors like John Wayne. It's like the sheriff was in town. He proceeded to sit at the head of the table and went around asking each individual to say something about what went wrong during the year and offer any incidents that he should know about. When it came around to me, Steinbrenner said, "Mangold, what's this I hear about Giambi coming out late to practice or stretch sometimes?"

I just thought to myself, *I'm not going to contradict or argue with The Boss.* I noted Jason Giambi might have done that a few times. "And whose fault is that?" The Boss asked.

I started to offer up that it was my fault, and he quickly interrupted and shot back: "No, it's not your fault. That's Torre's fault! Discipline starts from the top. Don't worry. We're going to get this taken care of."

That was all he had for me. It still was shocking to hear him question Torre to me, especially when that wasn't the manager's responsibility. Everyone heard rumors that Steinbrenner didn't like how much credit Torre got when we won, but that was my first time experiencing that directly. That was quite a meeting. We were there probably an hour and a half, maybe two hours. Steinbrenner eventually broke it up, but he said to me something to the effect of, "Mangold, I need you to get back over to the complex to prep for player visits during the winter. We need to streamline some things and change certain workouts. Why don't you head on back there? Here, you can take my car."

Steinbrenner stayed at the restaurant with a few others, and I headed over to the complex with Russell Orr, who was a strength and conditioning assistant at the Tampa complex and later went on to work in that capacity at Florida State. I didn't really want to drive Steinbrenner's car, so Orr drove. As soon as he started it up, the music was blaring from what Steinbrenner had been listening to before he arrived. It was a CD of the Ohio State fight song. Steinbrenner hailed from Ohio, and that must have been the week that Ohio State was going to play Michigan or another Big Ten rival, and so he had fight song on a CD cranked up to the max. I think he must have been getting ready to blister some people at this meeting and was apparently listening to the Buckeyes' fight song to get himself pumped up. I guess that's why he was running a few minutes late.

Yogi, Billy, and Sweet Lou

ONE THING I LEARNED RIGHT AWAY UPON ARRIVAL WITH THE NEW York Yankees in 1984 was that all of the players respected Yogi Berra like crazy, and why wouldn't they? He had accomplished everything in baseball. A Hall of Fame player, he was a beloved icon of the game and enjoyed success as a respected coach and manager with the Yankees and other teams, including taking the New York Mets to the World Series in 1973.

Other than that aforementioned dugout phone cord story with George Steinbrenner in the previous chapter, I don't have many wacky personal anecdotes to share about Yogi from my first year in the Bronx. He didn't say much and wasn't really hands-on with a lot of in-game advice, but he definitely was a players' manager. We won 87 games that year, but the Detroit Tigers opened the season red hot, going 35–5, and they ran away with the American League East division in the days before there were wild-card teams, leading us by 17 games.

The craziness involving Berra occurred the following year, of course. Steinbrenner had stated over the winter that Yogi was going to have the whole year in 1985—and then he fired him 16 games into the season as the Yankees had a 6–10 record. To be a part of that, to see a man of Yogi's stature treated that way was, really an eye-opener for me. His son Dale even was on the team, too, that year.

The grumbling and the rumblings started early on. We flew into Chicago for a three-game weekend series against the White Sox beginning April 26th. The word was if we didn't take two of three, Yogi was gone. On both Friday and Saturday, we got beat, and on a hot, dusty Sunday in Chicago we lost again 4–3. Steinbrenner had Clyde King, who was the first-year general manger in that ever-changing role, fly in to inform Yogi he was done. I know that's what angered Yogi and the coaching staff the most: that Steinbrenner didn't fire him personally. It led to a grudge that lasted nearly 15 years before No. 8 finally returned to Yankee Stadium in 1999.

I'll never forget being in the locker room after word came down that Yogi was gone and that Billy Martin would be taking over. The players just went crazy, kicking trash cans, cursing. Guys were just seething. Don Mattingly was very upset, throwing tape and other things. Veteran designated hitter Don Baylor also was really pissed off. Part of the emotion was directly because they loved Yogi so much, but I think it was also because Martin was coming back.

The shame about Yogi getting canned so early in the season was that he didn't really have all of his weapons to start that year. Rickey Henderson, the stolen base king we had acquired from the Oakland A's that winter, and Dave Winfield had been nursing injuries. I think a previous incident, in which Yogi had gotten upset with The Boss' meddling and flipped a pack of cigarettes at him during one of our spring training meetings in that trailer in Fort Lauderdale, Florida, always stuck with Steinbrenner. He may have been just looking for the first excuse to fire him.

From Chicago we had to fly to Texas to face the Rangers the next day. The clubhouse cleared out very quickly after the game. After coming in to talk to the guys for just a few minutes, the media was kicked out, and we all had changed into our suits because that was the protocol when we traveled. One TV crew tried to come back into the clubhouse, and Baylor stood at the door, saying, "That's it, guys, no more. We're done."

One of them made some smart ass comment like, "We're fine. Don't worry about us."

Baylor screamed back, "I said: get your asses out of here!" He immediately took off his watch and a big diamond bracelet on his other wrist as if to say, *If you don't leave, somebody's going down here.* A bunch of us had to hold him back, and the camera crews were told once again, "Guys, get out of here now, or somebody's going to get hurt." Baylor definitely was ready to kick some ass. Needless to say, the clubhouse was not reopened.

When we finally boarded the bus and went to O'Hare International Airport, Yogi actually was on the bus with us. We were going to fly Continental Airlines to Dallas, but he got off at the United terminal to head back to the East Coast. It was like it was a street stop on a bus in Brooklyn or something, like he just rang the bell and got off at a different stop. The bus slowed down and stopped, and Yogi just said, "Well, I'm getting off here, guys. You guys take care. I'm okay."

Here was Yogi Berra, one of the legendary names and figures in Yankees history and baseball history, getting off the team bus by himself and just going his separate way from the Yankees. *My God, can you imagine?*

Thus, we flew to Texas, and guys were putting away some beverages, that's for sure. We landed and boarded the bus to go to the hotel. After not really speaking much to the media in Chicago, you knew there was probably going to be tons of media waiting for us to get comments from the players about the transition. For some reason, there were no keys out in the lobby for the players to get to their rooms. Also, the elevators supposedly weren't working. So here you had a bunch of toasty players, still fuming from what had happened, and there were no elevators to board. These guys were stuck down there in the lobby for several minutes unless they wanted to take the stairs up to their rooms. I just grabbed my keys and looked around and left, but these guys were pretty much trapped in the lobby with all of these microphones in their faces. I would not have been surprised if Steinbrenner had orchestrated it. I always wondered if he did a little scheming here. It didn't seem like it was just a coincidence.

Either way, Tornado Billy touched down the next day. He already had been fired three times by Steinbrenner in 1978, 1979, and 1983 due to various off-field problems and incidents, and this would be his fourth of five stints as manager before he died tragically in a drunk-driving accident on Christmas of 1989. The team actually took off after Martin's arrival, finishing the '85 season with 97 wins but just two games behind the Toronto Blue Jays for the AL East division title. Once Henderson and Winfield got back in the lineup and the way Mattingly was hitting on his way to winning the MVP that year, we had tons of offensive talent—even if maybe we didn't really have enough pitching to win it all.

It probably took Martin and I a few days to talk after he replaced Yogi. I don't think he really even cared to meet me or vice versa. My mind-set was: just continue to do your job and don't ruffle any feathers. Just take care of business and stay out of the way. Don't do anything to start a fire or bring attention to yourself. I do recall the first time we spoke. During a batting practice, I went up and shook his hand. It was like his hand came out of a refrigerator or something. It was so cold, clammy, and boney. There were not many words exchanged at all. I told him to let me know if he needed something from me.

Bill Monboquette was a coach that year, but Martin forever was connected with Art Fowler, who'd served as his pitching coach with the Yankees in 1977–78 and in 1983 and also in other managerial stops with the Minnesota Twins, Detroit, Texas, and Oakland.

Fowler returned later in my first tenure with the Yankees when Martin came back for Round 5 in 1988. Wherever Martin would go, Fowler would be there. Those plastic tubs that you used at your lockers to soak your feet? Well, they always would have six packs of beer icing down in those basins. Right after the game, they'd always have beer waiting for them. Fowler was somebody that Martin trusted at various stops along the way and actually was a funny guy. Always red in the face, he definitely was Martin's drinking buddy.

One blowup I had with Martin came in spring training of the 1988 season when rookie infielder Randy Velarde somehow had hurt his shoulder and had to be held out of an exhibition game. Velarde was a true physical specimen, one of the early guys in baseball who really enjoyed working out. (He later admitted to getting involved with performance-enhancing drugs.)

Word got to Martin that Velarde might have hurt his shoulder working out. After the game, we were in the clubhouse in Fort Lauderdale, and I saw Martin just kind of looking around and pacing like he was really on a mission to find somebody.

All of a sudden, I just had this feeling that he was looking for me. Sure enough, he saw me, locked eyes with me, and came storming over to where I was. He probably caught me right where he wanted to, right in the middle of the clubhouse. He came up to me and started poking his fingers in my chest in front of everyone, going, "God dammit, we lost a player because he was working out in the weight room. Velarde can't play tonight. He's a very important part of this team and he can't play because he hurt himself in there using those damn weights. I don't want anyone using these weights ever again. Got me?"

At first you think, *Oh man, what are we going to do? A ban from training.* I knew I had to let it slide a little and just get going again. I guess I kind of learned quickly with Martin that you just took these things with a grain of salt. Take your lashings and then move on. I think Martin probably forgot all about it soon thereafter, but you always had to be looking over your shoulder for him. His competitiveness was unmistakable.

When Mattingly was at the plate during the 1985 season, Martin and Earl Weaver, the fiery Hall of Fame manager of the Baltimore Orioles, were screaming at the umpire. It was a close game, and Mattingly was working the count. The umpire was kind of squeezing him. You could see that Mattingly was getting agitated and really just wanted to get a feel for the strike zone. Weaver was screaming his lungs out across the way, and Martin was bitching right back at him. I don't even remember what it was about, but Mattingly was getting more and more aggravated at the umpire, and all of the yelling couldn't have helped calm the situation. These guys were just not letting up on each other. Finally, and this was kind of the greatness of Mattingly, he drove a double up the alley in right-center. I remember he took a step or two toward first base, turned around, and looked at the ump as if to say, "You really made me work for this, and to hell with you."

During that same 1985 season, Martin broke his arm in that fistfight with Yankees pitcher Ed Whitson, a big free-agent signing who ended up being the poster boy for players being unable to succeed in New York. We were in Baltimore, staying at the Cross Keys Inn. I didn't see any of it, but I did hear some of it. I was in my room. Scott Bradley, one of our catchers, was with me. We were watching a college football game, and all of a sudden, Bradley ran out of the room when we heard this big commotion going on. I didn't go out to see what happened. I was planning to call it a night and get up and have a good day the next day. It ended up being the night Martin and Whitson had their big run-in at the bar.

I remember the next day very well. It was less than an hour before our game in Baltimore. We already held our batting practice and everything, and there was still no lineup posted. Guys were wondering what was going on. All of a sudden, Martin stumbled in, sporting his cowboy boots, black jeans, and the cast. He just looked horrible. He had to put together a lineup real quick. This was late September right before the season ended. Martin ended up getting fired again by Steinbrenner right after the season ended, even though we finished only two games behind the Blue Jays in the division.

Martin's other memorable fight when I was there came in Texas in 1988. He was at a strip club and supposedly got beat up by three guys in the bathroom. I had gone out with some college friends after our game that night against the Rangers and come back to the hotel. I walked into the lobby and I could see behind the counter and the check-in area that there were these offices. The door was open, and it just so happened there was Martin lying on a table, and he had a white blanket over three-quarters of his body, and there was blood on the sheet.

Martin had been out with Mike Ferraro, one of our coaches. They'd been drinking at the hotel bar with Hall of Famer and Yankees legend Mickey Mantle, Martin's old teammate and pal who lived nearby in Texas. After Mantle went home, Martin wound up at this topless establishment with Ferraro called Lace. He claimed that three guys jumped him in the bathroom. I'm sure things were said leading up to that, and it wasn't as innocent as Martin made it seem.

The next day was a televised game against the Rangers, and before the game, Martin, who had around 40 stitches in his ear from the fight, came up to me and said, "Listen, big TV game today, you know these cameras are going to be trying to get all over me. I want you to stand in front of that camera as much as you can to keep those cameras off me," he told me. "That's your job today. Keep those cameras off me."

I don't know how well I performed that task, but once again, Steinbrenner had enough with Martin and fired him for a fifth time less than a month after that incident. Lou Piniella, who had been a player/coach my first year in 1984 and the manager in 1986–87 before being promoted to the front office, took over for his second tenure in the dugout.

I learned about Piniella's competitiveness and personality right from my first spring training camp with the team in 1984. Near the end of practice, we were doing running drills, and Piniella was never in great shape nor was he exactly known as Mr. Speed. There were fans in the stands off the right-field foul line, as everyone wanted to get up close to the Yankee players. I was having the players do interval sprints, where they would sprint 30 to 40 yards, then walk back to the beginning, and then go again. The fans kept yelling for Piniella, Rick Cerone, Butch Wynegar, Baylor, Ken Griffey Sr., and others. Probably because Piniella was coming in last all the time and looked like he was about ready to die, some fan yelled, "Hey, Piniella, what the hell are you doing? Come on, get moving!" Finally we finished, and I circled these players up just to stretch and cool down. This one fan kept riding Piniella, saying, "You keep coming in last, you can't even touch your toes."

And then Piniella finally had enough, and fired back, "I'll tell you what I'm doing, I'm sucking on your mother's tits!" And then while laughing, he turned to me and said, "I told that son of a bitch, huh?"

As a manager Piniella was so fiery, such a competitor. He hated to lose or to get embarrassed. One time we were in Kansas City to play the Royals. It was a day game and was boiling hot on the artificial turf of Royals Stadium, and we were getting hammered. Kevin Seitzer was one of their good, young players and later went on to become a big league hitting coach. In the seventh or eighth inning, Seitzer was complaining and yelling at the umpire about balls and strikes. Piniella just started yelling across the field, "Shut the fuck up! It's 11–0, and you're complaining about this shit? Shut up, you asshole. Go sit down!"

As you probably can tell, it rarely was dull having these three colorful baseball lifers—Yogi, Martin, Piniella, Martin again, and Piniella again—as the managers during my first five years with the Yankees. Just like them, my first run with the organization was about to end—even if my story in baseball really was only beginning.

Mattingly and
the Other Stars
of the '80s

DURING THE 1980S THE NEW YORK YANKEES HAD ALL-STARS LIKE DON Mattingly, Dave Winfield, and Rickey Henderson, and any one of those guys could carry a team for long stretches of a season. If they were all hitting on the same cylinders at the same time, forget about it. Don Baylor also was a former MVP with the California Angels and was as professional a hitter as I've ever witnessed up close on a regular basis. Henderson easily could have been the American League MVP in 1985 when Mattingly won it. Out of the leadoff spot, Henderson had 146 runs scored, 24 homers, and 80 stolen bases. If that team had any pitching at all, they could have won it all.

Watching Mattingly play every day was impressive. His day-in-and-day-out approach was something that I'd never seen. "I'm a professional, and you can't take a day off. If it's 98 degrees in Chicago, a day game after a night game, and the dust is all up in your face," he told me, "I'm going to be out there giving it my all for the people who come watch us play. You only have so much time to play this game."

Mattingly was a small-town Midwest guy, just like me. But he took to New York right away, and the city definitely loved him back and appreciated him. Mattingly always seemed to hit the ball on the sweet spot of the bat. He always hit the ball hard. He'd never get cheated and would make tremendous contact. In 1984 we were playing a home game, and Mattingly came into the dugout after making an out. I was seated on the bench, and he walked a few steps and stopped to take off his batting gloves. I was within easy earshot of him, and he quietly proclaimed that the next time up, the pitcher was going to try to "sneak a piece of cheese" by him on the inside of the plate, which in layman's terms meant a fastball on the hands. "I'm going to take him deep," Mattingly said.

Sure enough, he homered off him.

I remember the first time I saw him take batting practice, I told my parents, "This guy, Mattingly, is going to be something special." We opened the 1984 season in Kansas City my first year, and my parents had driven down from Sioux City, Iowa, which was about a six-hour drive to Royals Stadium. For the opening game, my parents happened to sit next to the Mattinglys in the stands and spoke with them throughout the game. Don's parents mentioned how their family was similar to ours, how when Donnie was a kid, he'd play with his brothers—baseball, basketball, whatever it was. That was the same thing I did with my siblings. Similarly, they were all very competitive even within the family. My father told Donnie's dad, "Your son is quite the player, quite the hitter."

Mrs. Mattingly interjected, "You should have seen our other son."

When Don Mattingly was eight years old, his older brother Jerry died in a highway construction accident in Indiana. I never spoke to Donnie about that. He actually wore No. 23 for the Yankees because his brother was 23 years old when he died.

As for Winfield and Baylor, as great as they were as ballplayers, I'll never forget how those two guys took out 19-year-old pitcher Jose Rijo for a new wardrobe when he first was brought up to New York in 1984. Rijo was a spectacular talent, but George Steinbrenner wanted him brought up because the New York Mets were getting all these headlines for having 19-year-old Doc Gooden starring at that age across town. Steinbrenner demanded: "Who do we have in the minors that we can bring up?"

Well, that was Rijo. He went on to quite a nice career after the Yankees traded him to the Oakland A's in the Henderson deal. But he wasn't ready yet on the mound at 19 to be in the major leagues and he definitely wasn't ready off the field. The poor kid showed up with this sport coat that came barely past his elbows. He had no money and was just this young kid pitching only a few games above Single A ball. Winfield took him out and bought him some nice dress clothes. Baylor, whom I became very close to, always looked out for him, too. I was very fond of Baylor. He was such a professional.

The difference between the players in that era of the mid-to-late '80s was that they would not only take care of the young rookies, but also the staff. If I would walk into a restaurant with Dom Scala, who was our bullpen catcher, the players would not let us pay the bill. If they were around, they always picked up the check. When we were leaving spring training in '84, we were having our cars shipped up to New York. When we got to Yankee Stadium for some reason, the truck that had my car on it got delayed. Baylor heard about this and he came over to me without making a big show of it. He tossed me a set of keys. "What's this?" I asked him.

"My car is in the lot, spot No. 25 [his uniform number]. Take my car," he said. "I don't need it, I have plenty of cars. Use it for as long as you need it."

I went out there, and it was this beautiful four-door Mercedes. I got into it, and on the dashboard ingrained in a plaque, it said "Specially designed for The Groove, Don Baylor." The Groove was his nickname.

I was staying at the Ramada Inn, one of our team hotels, in Paramus, New Jersey. The first time I had his car, I drove up the Major Deegan Expressway in the Bronx to get to the George Washington

Bridge to New Jersey. I got on the ramp, but I got caught not knowing whether to take the upper or lower level. I didn't really know which one I was supposed to take. I ended up driving straight ahead and stopping where they have those big containers of sand for crashes that you see sometimes. I just eased right into that area and came to a dead stop. Cars were zooming by on both sides to go to either the upper or lower levels of the bridge. My heart was pounding. I was panicking. I had Baylor's car and I was trying to figure out what to do. At least I didn't get hit. I didn't ever tell Baylor about it, but the fact that he allowed me to take his car for a few days was pretty cool of him. I mean, how many guys would just give you their car without making a big show of it? He barely knew me at that point.

Baylor always talked about how Frank Robinson was his mentor. Robinson always told him how to play hard, how to go into second base, and how to carry himself off the field.

When Baylor was a young guy with the Baltimore Orioles, he had it all. He was fast, he hit for power, he could steal bases, and he'd go hard into second base and take people out. He was a no-nonsense guy. He was a heck of a hitter and a heck of a leader.

Winfield was another guy that I, along with my family, had a special relationship with through the years. He had his charitable foundation, the David M. Winfield Foundation, which is why my wife and I always referred to him as David. This, of course, was the foundation that Steinbrenner was trying to dig up dirt on with that gambler, Howie Spira, and it resulted in The Boss being suspended by Major League Baseball for a few years. It was a foundation for underprivileged youths and had a drug awareness program for inner-city and impoverished kids. Until retiring in 2020, my wife Gale worked as a students' assistance counselor for many years in New Jersey and helped high school kids who had issues with addiction, drugs, alcohol, child abuse, and domestic violence. During our early years with the Yankees, Gale had heard about Winfield's foundation and she told him that she wanted to get involved. She ended up doing some great work with him and his foundation, assisting him in different projects. I think he felt a mutual respect for us because of that. I've seen him a few times over the years since he retired in 1995 and was elected to the Hall of Fame in 2001.

One time during my second stint with the Yankees in the late 1990s or the early 2000s, Winfield came into the clubhouse, where you had all these younger stars like Derek Jeter, Tino Martinez, Bernie Williams, and so on. One of the first people that Winfield came up to and said hello to was me. That was a moment of pride, and I felt great respect from him because of that. Here were all these up-and-coming stars, and Winfield went to come up to talk to a guy like me instead. I don't know if that's a feather in my cap or anything, but there was always such a mutual respect between us.

On the field Winfield had such an intimidating physical presence. He could hit a line drive as hard and far as anyone and throw a seed from the warning track in right field on a line to third base like no one else. What separated Winfield from others was his ability to turn a simple single into a double. He would bust his tail out of the box with his long stride, making a wide turn at first base, and you just knew he was not going to stop, hoping the outfielder would take his time charging the ball and throwing to second. By the time the outfielder realized Winfield was going to second, the outfielder would be so startled he would misfire or boot the ball. The only other comparable player with that daring helmet-bouncing-off-their-head, galloping style was a young Kirk Gibson when he was with the Detroit Tigers.

Henderson was a different kind of dude and famously kind of spacy. He always talked to his bat. He would sit on the bench with the handle between his knees and he'd talk into the barrel, going, "Come on, Rickey, what the hell are you doing?" He'd always refer to himself in the third person.

When we were in Minnesota to play the Twins, our radio broadcaster John Gordon wanted Henderson to read a commercial. It didn't go too well. Eventually he just stormed off and said, "I'm not doing this."

Still, what an unbelievable athletic specimen he was. He also was a highly-sought-after running back in the Bay Area, and that's why he and Billy Martin were so tight. They had been together with the Oakland A's in the beginning of the 1980s. Henderson always played hard for Martin. They definitely took care of each other. If there was any doubt about whether Henderson didn't run out a ball or if a ball dropped in front of him, I think Martin would give him a little leeway. Henderson would have some moments like that, but he also was so spectacular on the field. You definitely took the good with the bad with him, and there was far more good than bad when he was healthy. He was just ripped and so physically gifted.

By that time in my second season, I had started getting these guys to train and to work out in specific programs. Henderson had worked out some earlier in his career but not consistently nor really hard. He just had such vascularity, and his body fat was under 5 percent. That was just his natural athletic build. His quads, hamstrings, and glutes were why he moved so fast. He was the poster boy for fast-twitch muscle fiber. He was just so explosive. When he was stealing a base, he would take his first step and then he was just gone. He'd get down low in that wide stance just like Lou Brock did. Staying low and gradually coming up is what all great sprinters do. They don't stand straight up right away. He was the opposite of someone like Bernie Williams, who also had the physical gifts but wasn't mechanically or instinctively as polished as a base runner.

Baylor wasn't much of a workout guy either, but he was another guy who just naturally was strong. During my 17 years in Major League Baseball, guys would shave down the handle of their bat to have a little more whip, a little more bat speed through the strike zone. Baylor was so strong that I once saw him break his bat on a check swing without making contact with the ball. Do you know how strong you have to be to do that? To be able to stop, start, and crack the bat at the handle on a partial swing is just sheer power. It's like a Mike Tyson punch.

Baylor was in his mid-30s by then, but I give him credit for the work he put in with me to try to increase his flexibility. He was just so muscular, especially his hamstrings and his back. So he always tried to stretch. He was definitely smart enough to understand it was going to be a positive for him. Steinbrenner also was a stickler for body weight when it came to Baylor, who wasn't overweight at all in my estimation, just really solid and powerful. Steinbrenner mandated that me and our head trainer, Gene Monahan, keep track of the body weights of the players. "Baylor has to be weighed in every day," he said.

We were in Oakland for a day game after a night game, and guys were slowly rolling through in the morning after a short night, and I had to weigh in Baylor before the game. I went to his locker, and we got into an argument about it. "Come on, George wants this," I said. "We've got to get this done."

He fired back at me: "Get lost. Tell George to go screw himself. Put down whatever you want as my weight."

He finally did it because I was persistent enough. Toward the end of his career, maybe he battled his weight, but he wasn't fat. He had a large muscular stomach area. It was thick. It was kind of abnormal and gave the illusion that he was fat. But he wasn't.

Another thing about Baylor was that he regularly led the league in getting hit by pitches. He just stood in there and took it. He just would turn his big shoulder into the ball. When he got hit, he never rubbed his bruised body part. He just would lay the bat down and go down to first.

On the flipside, he had a very soft side, too. I have a tremendous picture of him with my wife and I at a downtown New York steakhouse. He was a spokesman for Cystic Fibrosis because his son Donnie had the disease. Baylor had invited my wife and I to this dinner, and it was an honor to participate in it with him.

Baylor played only three of his 19 seasons with the Yankees, and Winfield and Henderson were first-ballot Hall of Famers as much for what they accomplished elsewhere in their careers than what they did for the Yankees. I know the homegrown guys from the organization always held a more special place in the hearts and eyes of the fans.

Ron Guidry, like Donnie Baseball, was one of those players. Beyond all of the accolades, and everybody knows about Guidry's pitching prowess, he was quiet, yet personable. He could sit there on the bench for a whole game and not say a word. He would just sit there with his Skoal Bandits and just lean forward, spit, and watch the game. He was content just to be there on the days he wasn't pitching. I was right there for a day game at Yankee Stadium when Richie Garcia was the home-plate umpire. He's known as being a real red ass, having big ears, hearing things all the time that were said in the dugout, and not letting things go.

Tim Foli, one of our infielders, and Gator—but mostly Foli—got into it with Garcia before the game even began. We had a whole bag of balls, which were rubbed up for use in the game, sitting on the dugout steps to be given to the umpire. Foli kept yelling out, "These things are too dark! They can't be used."

It started out like he was just joking around with Garcia, but then they started really yelling at each other. Foli was a hothead anyway, but so was Garcia, and then Gator chimed in and injected himself into the conversation. I was seated right by these guys, and finally before the national anthem had even played, Garcia walked over and said, "Somebody in this dugout has got to go. I'm not taking this shit from you guys all day."

And Gator pops up and goes, "Okay, Richie, I'm outta here. I'm gone." He wasn't supposed to pitch that day anyway. He was just going to be relaxing on the bench. So he volunteered for the ejection.

Guidry also was such a big-time athlete. As far as testing and evaluation of the players, I really hadn't had a chance to institute that yet in my first year. Evaluating speed, explosive power, and strength took time. I recognize the true athletes when I see them perform, and Guidry was so electric. He didn't weigh more than 170 pounds, but he could generate such force and throw in the low-to-mid-90s. He also fielded his position the way he did because he was so quick. He always had that bounce to him. When he pitched, he had that little recoil to his delivery. He had such fast-twitch muscle fiber, too, where his muscles could contract at such a high rate of speed. That's how the fast and explosive players could generate bat or arm speed.

You just knew by watching him that Gator was very talented and blessed athletically. That's not really something you could teach. Three-quarters of that is hereditary. It's your genes, your physical makeup. You can train to improve your explosive power, but when your muscle fiber is set up to where it's predominantly fast-twitch fiber, you're going to be able to generate more power and speed. People always said that about Mariano Rivera, too. He was such a terrific natural athlete that he could have been a great outfielder.

Just like Rivera did, Guidry would man center field and just run down ball after ball so fluidly during batting practice. He enjoyed doing that and would make some of the most unbelievable catches and cover such ground. People worried that he would collide with someone or run into a wall or something. He always said he got his conditioning in by running hard and running down balls.

I was gone by the time Rivera tore his ACL in 2012 while doing that out in Kansas City, but it looked like he kind of slipped on the warning track and injured himself. Rivera and Guidry were very similar in their physical makeup. Long limbed and lean, they still had fast-twitch, explosive muscle fiber. They both could've been great wide receivers or defensive backs. They were just unbelievable and natural.

Reggie Jackson had left the Yankees by the time I arrived. He signed with the California Angels in 1982 after five eventful seasons in the Bronx. I met Jackson for the first time in 1984 when he returned with the Angels to Yankee Stadium for a weekend series. I was out early on Friday working out on the field, going through a circuit of running and performing exercises at three different stations. One station was jumping rope with a special jump rope called a "Heavy Rope."

Jackson also was out early doing some light running. He asked me about the rope and inquired about how to get one. I went out and bought one on Saturday and had it sent to the visitors' clubhouse. He said he would pay me the $100 that it cost. I never received the money that weekend, but the following week, we visited the Angels in Anaheim. I wanted my money. I went to the home clubhouse to track down Jackson. When I walked into their clubhouse, Mr. October was being interviewed by Dick Enberg, which was pretty cool as a big sports fan. Jackson spotted me while he was talking to Enberg and he signaled for me to wait. He then paid me back what he owed me.

That always was one of the coolest things about being associated with the Yankees. You never knew who you might meet at the ballpark or at outside events related to the team. Legends like Joe DiMaggio, Mickey Mantle, Whitey Ford, and so many names who were synonymous with the pinstripes and Yankee lore were around regularly, and you'd get to meet them at Old-Timers' Day every year, which was a big thrill for someone who revered the game the way I did as a boy.

Since I was a die-hard St. Louis Cardinals fan growing up in the Midwest, meeting Roger Maris, who finished his career with the Cardinals (1967–68) six years after breaking Babe Ruth's single-season home run record with 61 in 1961, was a huge thrill. The Yankees were retiring Maris' number at Old-Timers' Day in July 1984, and right after the ceremony, I came into the food room to grab a quick sandwich and a drink before showering up and getting ready for our game. Nobody else was in the room because our batting practice was still taking place. All of a sudden, Maris was behind me. He shut the door, and his shoulders dropped down in relief. It was just like everyone said: he always wanted privacy. Even to that day, he was tired of being interviewed and hounded and pestered. He also had been diagnosed with Non-Hodgkin's lymphoma the year before. He would die from the disease at 51 in December 1985. I introduced myself to him, and he and I spoke for a few minutes about my job. "Strength and conditioning is a very important part of the game," Maris said. "I used to work out a little bit. I knew the importance of staying strong."

Then we talked about his time with the Cardinals, my boyhood team, and how part of his contract with the Cards was that down near Tampa, Florida, where he lived, he had part ownership of a Budweiser brewery from the Busch family in St. Louis. Our chat lasted five-to-seven minutes at the most, but it was great. It meant so much to me. Just to spend a bit of time alone chatting with Maris, one of my idols, was incredible. He wished me continued good luck and said, "You guys have a great team and continued success."

The '80s

DEREK JETER ONCE MADE A CAMEO IN A BUDDY COP COMEDY ENTITLED *The Other Guys*, in which he gets shot by a police officer played by Mark Wahlberg. This chapter is my version of *The Other Guys* from my first several years in New York. It's replete with several cameos or funny anecdotes about some of the less famous New York Yankees of the 1980s.

Joe Cowley, for instance, was this young, talented right-handed pitcher, but he was just a total goofball, very cocky, and rubbed some people the wrong way. In spring training of 1984, he was all set with his red Corvette that he used to drive around Fort Lauderdale, Florida. One of his teammates—I wish I remembered who—had the highway patrol come in one day to the clubhouse. Two of the officers came in and handcuffed Cowley. They said they'd seen him numerous times speeding around town and driving recklessly and that they had to take him outside to talk to him about breaking the law. Everybody knew it was a prank, but it was funny to watch it all go down. The highway patrolmen did a great job of acting and going along with the gag. I don't know if Cowley got put in the cruiser, but I think a few minutes after they got him outside, they told him it was a joke and let him go. They definitely cuffed him. Cowley only pitched five years in the majors, but befitting his personality, he threw a no-hitter with seven walks for the Chicago White Sox in 1986.

Another guy, Toby Harrah, was this old-school, hard-core type infielder who had been successful earlier in his career with the Cleveland Indians and the Texas Rangers. The Yankees acquired him past his prime, and that was done too often then: bringing in players who were past their expiration date. It just never worked for Harrah in New York. He didn't enjoy the big city and didn't like life with the Yankees. He got off to a bad start in 1984 and never caught his stride. He heard the boos and he just couldn't handle it. It just went downhill quickly, and he finished the season hitting just .217. Harrah and Cowley also didn't get along at all. They had very different approaches to life. Harrah ended up going back to Texas after just one year with the Yanks.

When he was back with the Rangers, he returned to Yankee Stadium in '85 and hit a slow roller down the first-base line. Cowley was pitching and he fielded it in plenty of time. He wasn't going to toss it to first base but was just going to tag Harrah out. Harrah always played hard and always ran hard down to first base. Because he couldn't stand Cowley, he just threw his shoulder into his former teammate's face when the pitcher came over to tag him. I don't know if he broke his nose, but he definitely bloodied him up. Cowley went down, and the trainers ran out there, and that white towel sure turned red very quickly. Cowley, being the goofball that he is, threw his arm up and started waving to everybody in the crowd, signaling that he was okay. I know Harrah was probably smiling, too, thinking, *I got his ass.*

There also was Phil Niekro, the Hall of Fame knuckleballer and a 318-game winner in the majors who passed away in 2020. He was 45 by 1984 and he pitched a few more years until he was 48. He actually went 16–8 with the Yankees in '84, pitched 215 innings, and had a 3.09 ERA. One day we were out on the field, and he was laying on the ground and stretching, and I said, "Knucksie, what is the key to your success and being able to pitch at your age? I'm curious what you do."

He answered very matter of factly: "Well, I eat when I'm hungry and I sleep when I'm tired."

Niekro kind of smirked and turned his head like he didn't want to say more, but it was hard to argue with the success that he had well into his 40s. He also was from Lansing, Ohio. We were in Cleveland at the old Municipal Stadium there, the so-called "Mistake by the Lake." He was a very good, lifelong friend of John Havlicek, the Hall of Fame forward from the Boston Celtics. Havlicek came into the clubhouse one time to see Niekro. They grew up together and went to the same high school. That was a pretty cool connection.

Another one of my instant favorites was Dave Righetti, who had won Rookie of the Year as a starter three years earlier, but 1984 was his first year as the closer after Goose Gossage departed as a free agent. Rags was still a young guy, but he was such a natural-born leader, and that showed later in his long career with the San Francisco Giants as a pitching coach. He could relate to starters, to relievers, or somebody having that shining day of excellence because of the no-hitter he pitched against the Boston Red Sox on the Fourth of July in 1983.

He had really bad feet, and it was very difficult for him to run for conditioning work. I was getting on him at first, thinking he wasn't working hard. Getting to know him and seeing his feet and the pain that he was in quite a bit, I understood it better. At one point that year, *Sports Illustrated* did an article on the workouts we were doing. The relievers would gather with me during the final round of batting practice for conditioning work, some drills, some abdominal work, and some back work. *SI* called us the "Abdominal Showmen." We also did hip work and lateral leg raises. They were just some movements to keep their torsos—their cores—strong. This was mostly for the bullpen guys—Bob Shirley, Mike Armstrong, Jay Howell, a few others—and the guys that weren't pitching that day. Righetti was the man. Whatever he would do, guys would follow.

Rick Cerone, one of our catchers, was hilarious and had this dry sense of humor. Nobody was off limits for him to tease—not even Kansas City Royals outfielder Jim Eisenreich, who suffered from Tourette's Syndrome. In one case, he was even prophetic. We were in Texas in 1987 when Don Mattingly was about to tie the major league record for hitting a home run in eight consecutive games. We were all sitting on the bench, and Cerone stood up and said, "Listen guys, I'm not going to miss this. Donnie's gonna hit one right now. This is it."

Sure enough, one or two pitches later, Mattingly crushed one to left field to tie the record with Dale Long of the 1956 Pittsburgh Pirates. (The mark was later matched by Ken Griffey Jr. of the Seattle Mariners.) Mattingly had enough power to hit it out to the opposite field. That was one of the first times I remember hearing someone call a home run like that.

Cerone was the Yankees' starting catcher beginning in 1980, the year after Thurman Munson had died. He had left for the Atlanta Braves in 1985 and was gone for a couple of years before coming back to the Bronx in 1987. He was one of the slowest players that I ever coached. He tried hard, and I worked with him on improving his speed, but you can only do so much with guys who don't have that natural fast-twitch speed. With all the squatting behind home plate, most catchers are known for not being very fast. When I say he was slow, he was *slow*. He hit into an around-the-horn triple play in a 1984 game against the Minnesota Twins at Yankee Stadium. On a ground ball to third base, Gary Gaetti only had to take a step or two toward the bag, and immediately I knew this was going to be a triple play. Gaetti stepped on the bag as he fielded it, fired to second to

Tim Teufel, who turned it and threw to Kent Hrbek at first. Cerone was still two strides away from the bag. It wasn't even close at first.

This also was before they had mandated the ear flap on the batting helmet. Quite often, their helmets would go flying off when players would run. I'm sure fans can envision Dave Winfield legging out a double with his helmet flying off. Cerone ran down the first-base line with his left hand up, kind of holding his helmet on his head. I was thinking, *What is he doing? Just run.*

Cerone and I had several funny encounters involving running the bases. As a strength and conditioning coach, another big part of my focus was to try to help guys pick up a step or two while running the bases. Part of it was simply their first step out of the box. It has to be muscle memory because there is such an adrenaline flow when you're hitting and such excitement when you make contact, and then all of a sudden you have to start running at full speed. You have to have a certain flow and mechanics to it so that you do not tighten up in your legs, or your arms, or your fists. You also want to have that first stride headed down the first-base line and not toward the infield or toward the dugout. It's imperative to literally get yourself started in the right direction.

Running speed involves stride length, stride frequency, body lean, and arm action. It's a combination of trying to make your stride a little bit longer to cover more ground without losing the frequency of those strides. There are drills and mechanics to work on fundamentally correcting running and sprinting technique, and even someone who does not have the best speed can still increase his time.

My first year in 1984, I was so intent on running speed that I had a handheld tape recorder and a stopwatch in my hand all the time. I recorded everybody's time down the first-base line out of the box and kept track of that. It used to piss off our Cerone because he was a bit slow. Cerone got a hold of my recorder that I'd left on the bench. When I played it, it was him saying "Mangold, stick this recorder up your ass." When he saw me pick it up and press play, he started laughing.

Times definitely have changed in terms of technology and training equipment from when the Yankees first hired me in the 1980s to my latter years with the team. When I first got there, there were barely any facilities for road teams to use at the various ballparks. I actually had to travel in the beginning with this huge PVC pipe that I purchased with caps on each end, so that I was able to slide a lifting bar, which was seven feet long, and take it on the flights along with 80 to 100 pounds of weight plates.

We would work out in the shower areas sometimes and would use the wooden benches in there as a bench for bench presses. I also had a little box—about a 3' x 2' crate—and I would store some of the weights in there or I would set that little crate down so the players would lay down on that and hold the bar and do bench presses. When they were done, the next guy would lay down.

Rickey Henderson, Gary Ward, Dave Winfield, and others would pop in and just lift a little bit anywhere I could set up. The visiting clubhouses always were pretty tight, especially in the older stadiums like Tiger Stadium and Fenway Park. That was just how the game was. There was so much tradition and flavor to those older ballparks. To know so many players had come through there, you had to pinch yourself sometimes. But the lack of facilities definitely reflected the time periods those places were built.

Another Yankees catcher from those days was Butch Wynegar. We were in Milwaukee in July 1985 to face the Brewers, and Billy Martin was managing. Wynegar was one of those guys whose skin you could get under quite easily. He had to look over to the bench all the time for Martin's signals. That just wore on Wynegar, who was a tremendous young player. He felt disrespected. I don't think Martin liked him all that much. They just didn't get along for whatever reason. Not everybody got along with Martin anyway, but he liked to ride some guys and try to break them. He did that with Wynegar to the point it sent him into depression. Wynegar and I walked back to the hotel one night together, and he just said, "Jeff, I'm done, I'm quitting, I can't take this anymore." I asked him if he was serious, and Wynegar said, "Yeah, I don't need this anymore, I've had it. I'm going."

I didn't try to argue with him, just tried to communicate with him and be there for him, and sure enough, he wasn't around the next day. He had told the Yankees he was leaving the team in the middle of the season. He actually came back and played another couple of years after that for the California Angels in 1987 and 1988. That somewhat fits. New York is so unique. It's a very intense atmosphere with the Yankees—whether it be from management, the fans, or the media. Either you thrive with it, or it tears you apart and you can't handle it. Anaheim, California, is more laid-back. So that move made sense to me. He's from Pennsylvania and had played with the Twins before the Yankees. I was from the Midwest, so we had that in common. I have a very good memory with names and players and I was always speaking to him about different teammates, and he mentioned some of the suburbs of Minneapolis that were similar to where I grew up in Iowa. I think he just built a comfort zone with me.

As the strength and conditioning coach, you're with these players one on one quite a bit. Overall, part of my longevity in the major leagues was due to my ability of being a good listener and being able to understand these guys and the stresses they were under—whether it's family life, their ability to play, their worries, etc. Once a player trusts you to work with him physically, there's not much more trust that you can have in someone.

Dan Pasqua, a local kid from New Jersey, hit these thunderous bombs during batting practice, and people thought he was going to be the next Mickey Mantle. During one game in his rookie season of 1985, he was hitting barely .200 and was going up to pinch hit at Yankee Stadium. I was standing right near the bat rack, and he was kind of staring out, looking out over the crowd, and said, "Man, I can't hit here." I was thinking, *Wow, he's psyched out.* He had some marginal success the next couple of years and had a halfway decent career but very below what people thought he would have.

The Yankees traded him in 1987 to the White Sox, and he put up some okay numbers over there, but that early conversation stood out a lot to me. I think it was the pressure. I didn't ask him to elaborate on it. I wish I had, but at that point it was too late. Once you're thinking that way, once you get burned like that, it leaves a scar. I didn't think he was going to have success in New York, and he knew it in his head. He later admitted he put too much pressure on himself. He asked to be traded and went in the package in 1987 for right-handed pitcher Richard Dotson.

Ed Whitson, the same guy who had the brawl with Martin, was kind of the poster boy for a guy who signs a big contract in New York and just falls apart. He was a Tennessee country boy and he was just fish out of water, a deer in the headlights, the whole time. You could see it in his eyes. He just never was relaxed. He was on pins and needles the whole time. He was so out of place in New York that you almost felt sorry for him. On the days he was pitching at Yankee Stadium, Whitson would sit in this chair in the walkaway near the dugout and would go in to smoke a few cigarettes between innings. He asked me if I'd go up to the clubhouse and get him a Coke. I went back, and he reached out to take the soda, and his hand was shaking like you wouldn't believe. I was thinking, *This guy is going to try to go out there and pitch with his hand shaking like that?*

He told me once that his driveway was filled with tacks and nails. Somebody with a shotgun even had followed him home once. The fans, the media, and Martin, especially, were merciless with him, and he just couldn't ever get it together. He was overwhelmed. It got to the point where he wouldn't even walk across the field to warm up in the bullpen. He'd go through the underground hallway at Yankee Stadium just to not hear it from the fans. It was actually pretty sad. Some small-town guys thrive in New York, and some don't for whatever reason. In all my years with the Yankees, it was interesting to observe the new players—whether they were rookies coming up, trade acquisitions, or big free-agent signings. You just had to sit back and see how they were going to adjust. Could they handle it? Were they groomed for New York? For some of them, it totally elevated their game, and they loved the intensity. Others shrunk from within from that pressure.

Another guy who struggled in New York was Ken Phelps. The Yankees traded away Jay Buhner, a move which infamously infuriated Frank Costanza on *Seinfeld*. Everyone just knew that Buhner would be a player. But George Steinbrenner always was playing for today, always was impatient, and this was another impulsive move that blew up in his face. Phelps arrived midseason in 1988 and was gone by the next year. Like Buhner, Doug Drabek was another promising prospect who was traded away prematurely. You could just tell he was going to be a big-time pitcher. He was just a rookie in 1986. On the days he would not pitch, he was just a happy-go-lucky kid, a great personality. Drabek would drink as much coffee as he possibly could. Because of that he was known for always farting in the dugout. I'm sure he'd be pissed to read anything about that now, but he went on to a great career after the Yankees traded him away to Pittsburgh for Rick Rhoden in 1986. He even won a Cy Young Award in 1990.

Another player with Pittsburgh ties that gets forgotten from that time period was Rod Scurry, a lefty reliever who really had a hard time in New York. He had a troubled past, but I didn't see any drug problems from him when he was with the Yankees. He had been an excellent reliever for the Pirates, but when he came to the Yankees, he always had a very blank face. There was no emotion, no smiling, no laughing. It seemed like so many guys who came from Pittsburgh with that whole drug investigation there in 1982 had really been chewed up. (Scurry died in 1992 of a cocaine-related heart attack out in Las Vegas.)

There were a couple of lesser-known middle infielders from those Yankees teams in the 1980s with interesting backstories. One was Lenn Sakata, a Hawaiian with these big glasses who played with us for just 19 games in 1987. He suffered a career-ending injury in June of that season, tearing ligaments in his ankle while sliding back into second base on a pickoff throw.

Head athletic trainer Gene Monahan was out on field at second base attending to Sakata when he signaled that he needed the stretcher. No one came forward at this point to bring the stretcher out on the field, so Ron Kittle, an outfielder and designated hitter for us who had won Rookie of the Year for the White Sox in 1983, and I came forward to do so. The stretcher was always at the ready, hanging on the wall down the walkway to the ground crew cubby hole. Kittle and I were both physical guys and we came forward to go on field when no one intervened. We helped Sakata onto the stretcher, and we walked off the field with him. As we got over toward the first-base camera wall and the dugout to leave the field, Kittle ended up hurting his neck by going down the stairs awkwardly while carrying this stretcher. Like I feared, he ended up on the disabled list and ended up on the Indians the next season.

Another time we were in Milwaukee, and shortstop Wayne Tolleson was hitting against the Brewers. He was a scrappy little hitter, and I remember him for wearing No. 2 a few years before Derek Jeter arrived. Tolly had a propensity for fouling balls off, especially the other way. He was a switch-hitter, but he was up there left-handed, and we were in the visiting dugout on the third-base side. You always had to keep your eyes peeled for foul balls because most stadiums had no fences or screens protecting the dugouts at that time. Tolleson hit a screaming demon right over our dugout. The sound it made when it reached the stands was that of a plate of glass that got shattered. Guys jumped up and looked over the dugout, and this middle-aged man was just sitting there, and all of a sudden, blood started gushing from his mouth. I looked up really quick, and it was like a faucet opened up. The man fell flat on top of our dugout. Blood actually was dripping out of him and over the edge into our dugout. Our trainer, Gene Monahan, hopped up there and tried to help him, and all of a sudden, the guy looked up and started yelling for Mattingly. "Mattingly, I just wanted to shake your hand!"

This guy's face just exploded, his teeth everywhere, and he's talking about meeting Mattingly? Always a good guy, Mattingly shook his hand, and we all got a laugh out of it. It's a good thing they finally have those nets up now, especially with people on their phones all the time. I've seen too many people—kids and adults—get hit in those first four or five rows. You have absolutely no time to react if a ball comes.

Jack Clark was another guy who used to hit absolute rockets. He was only in New York for one year in 1988, but he'd been on the St. Louis Cardinals when they made the World Series twice in the previous three years. For a big, strong guy, he used the smallest bat, like a 31–32 ouncer with a thin handle. He swung so hard. There were no half swings with Jack; he was so dynamic and forceful and generated such bat speed. I remember he drove in 93 runs for us that season, but he hit just .246 with runners in scoring position. If he would have had just a normal year for him, he easily could have driven in 140. There were so many runners stranded that it just boggles the mind.

Lou Piniella was the manager in the second half of 1988 after Martin was canned again, and Piniella had a pregame meeting. He asked the guys to pull it together, saying the Yankees were better than they were playing. At the end of the meeting, Piniella told the guys, "If anybody has anything to say, now is the time."

There were a couple of seconds of silence, and then Clark said, "Yeah, I got a problem. I come to the ballpark every day and I don't know what I'm doing, if I'm DH-ing one day, first base another day, sometimes I'm in the outfield."

He was just challenging Piniella, who said, "Well, Jack, you're in the lineup, and you're getting your at-bats."

Clark countered that players wanted to know what they're going to be doing each day to prepare. "There's no rhyme or reason what's going on around here," he said, "the way I'm getting moved around." I understand that Clark was known for being vocal, but that showed me he would definitely speak up for himself and he wasn't afraid of anybody—not even Piniella.

John Candelaria also was a different type of guy. The left-handed pitcher grew up in Brooklyn and had been around the game a while. He definitely had an edge to him. He also had endured some real family-related tragedy when his two-year-old son died following a swimming pool accident in 1985. One day at Yankee Stadium, we were supposed to be out on the field for batting practice, but Candelaria was in the clubhouse with his feet up on the table smoking a cigarette. I said, "Candy, we gotta get going."

"I ain't doing shit today," he said. I believe it might have been his son's birthday.

Candy and I didn't always get along. During spring training in Fort Lauderdale, we were out in right field, the sun was shining bright, and I was out shagging fly balls during batting practice. Candelaria was maybe 20 feet from me when someone hit a rocket. You could just tell by the sound of the bat that it was smoked. I really couldn't see it or pick it up. You usually could see players turn a bit and follow the path of the ball and sense if it was coming your way. Candy, though, could see it. Then, I heard this thing zip by my head. I realized Candelaria was only a few feet away from me and didn't say "heads up" or anything. It felt like he was hoping that I would get hit. I looked at him, and he just shrugged, like, "Big deal." We didn't have any words about that after that incident, but sometimes words don't need to be spoken. There are just looks on faces that are enough. I knew he didn't like me.

Another lefty starter that I'll never forget was Al Leiter. His major league debut came in September of 1987. I always would get to the ballpark early and run and do a lot of stadium steps around Yankee Stadium. Leiter was a local kid from New Jersey and he was going to pitch that night against Milwaukee. He came out at the top of the steps by the on-deck circle. He took a look around all wide-eyed, and I could see him thinking, *Wow, this is where I'm gonna be tonight. I've made it.*"

Rex Hudler was another young player I was very fond of on those teams. He was a pure athlete. Notre Dame heavily recruited him as a wide receiver and quarterback, and you could see that athletic ability in him when he came up for a couple of short stints in 1984 and 1985. He was so energetic and gung-ho, a whatever-it-takes kind of a guy. If he had to run through a wall, he'd do it. He got a start in a spring training game at second base and was so excited. I had a way of getting guys like him fired up a little bit. "Let's go, Rex, let's play hard," I said. "This is where the fun starts."

He was so amped up that he grabbed the overhang of the dugout and he pulled off four or five one-arm chin-ups. He dropped down, landed on his feet, and said, "Yep, ready to go." What a guy. He always gave an all-out effort.

From 1986 to 1988, there was an on outfielder with us named Claudell Washington, who sadly died in June of 2020. In his first year with the team, we were out in Oakland, close to where he was from in northern California. Ever since he passed away, this story has been ingrained in my mind. I can see it plain as day. In the latter innings, Washington pinch hit for somebody and grounded out against Dave Stewart. I noticed Washington making his way up to the clubhouse. Later that same inning, Rickey Henderson, who was still playing for us and not the Oakland A's, pulled a muscle and had to come out of the game. Piniella was managing, and all of a sudden started calling for Washington. I ran up to the clubhouse and found Washington. He hadn't even showered, but he had his uniform off and was pulling his pants on. He figured he was out of the game and he was getting ready to take off for the day. "Claudell, you're still in the game," I said.

He looks at me like "Oh shit," and 10 to 15 seconds later Piniella came in. He actually didn't cuss him out or anything but said, "Claudell, you're in the game. Let's go." Maybe he yelled at him afterward, but Washington got dressed and got back out there.

In spring training of 1988, I was told Mike McCarthy was hired to assist me in the strength and conditioning program. Dan McCarthy was a Cleveland-based attorney and one of the minority owners of the Yankees. His son, Mike, was a big bodybuilder-looking guy, who was 6'3" or 6'4" and about 225 pounds. My first impressions of this guy was that something was not right with him.

There definitely was something shady going on there. It ended up being that he was a convicted felon.

Here's how I found out about it. During spring training we stayed at the Galt Ocean Mile Hotel in Fort Lauderdale, which is no longer around. Mike called me around dinner time one night, saying that he was kind of lonely and needed to talk to somebody and asked if I would I come to his room. I barely knew him, but I went down to his room, and he ended up telling me this story about how he had this girlfriend back in Cleveland who was a hooker, and her pimp beat the hell out of her.

It turns out that Mike was indicted in 1981 when he was 22 on an aggravated murder charge for killing the pimp named Tony Kittrell. Mike was charged with taking this pimp to a park in Cleveland, tying him to a tree, shooting him multiple times, and stabbing him more than 30 times. He ended up taking a plea for voluntary manslaughter rather than stand trial for murder and he was sentenced to seven to 20 years in prison. He only served three-and-a-half years and was paroled, and Steinbrenner was trying to do his partner a favor. He offered Mike a job with the Yankees at their minor league complex as a strength coach for their Single A affiliate. That meant he'd also be there in Fort Lauderdale working with me during spring training.

There was always something off about Mike even before the night he called me to his room. He always seemed like he was on something, whether it was steroids, cocaine, or other drugs. One night in 1989 after I'd left the Yankees, Mike was found by police and EMTs running naked on a Florida highway late at night after a game. He was transported to a local hospital, where he died of what was ruled a cocaine overdose.

The Boss, Joy, and Agony

HONESTLY, I'M STILL NOT EXACTLY SURE WHY MY FIRST TENURE WITH the New York Yankees ended. It certainly wasn't my doing. It was George Steinbrenner's. I just think he wanted to bring in somebody different, and that certainly was his prerogative. He'd fired more accomplished people than me through the years, that's for sure.

Bob Quinn was the general manager by that time, and when he informed me at the end of the 1988 season that I was being let go, it came as a complete shock to me. He called me into his office and said little more than "We're going to make a change." There was no further explanation. I tried to demand of Quinn to let me speak with Steinbrenner, but he would not let that come about. "Nope, I can't let you do that. It's not going to happen. I was told by George this is how it's going to be," Quinn told me.

I just let Quinn have it, "This is bullcrap. Let me talk to George."

I was insistent because I knew one thing: when Steinbrenner is one on one with somebody and he's not in front of a crowd, things were different. He could be Mr. Nice Guy and he would listen. If he was in a meeting or in front of other people, Steinbrenner was going to ridicule you, demean you, show his power, and never would back down.

Still, my feelings toward The Boss and my relationship with him were very positive. I think he liked that I had a football background and would do whatever he asked me to do. He also wouldn't let anything get in the way if he thought it was time to make a change. Dallas Green, the incoming manager after Billy Martin got axed one more time, didn't have anyone special in mind to replace me. I actually worked with Green later in my career with the New York Mets, and we got along well.

The Yankees brought in Gary Weil from Notre Dame, as Steinbrenner and former Notre Dame basketball coach Digger Phelps had a close relationship, and I think that combination was part of Weil's hiring. I remember Tommy John being upset about my firing. We had developed a strong relationship. Dave Winfield was, too.

I will say that it's probably true that I might not have been brought back to the Yankees a second time a decade later if I'd been given the chance to speak with Steinbrenner in 1988. I might have said some things I'd come to regret. In truth, though, I didn't have any regrets over my first five years in the Bronx. For the first time in a while, however, I needed to find a job. I continued to contact teams as much as possible, using whatever contacts I'd made, but nothing really was opening up on the professional level. I'd given thought to possibly working in the college ranks again, but for whatever reason, nothing really shook out for a while.

I began to train some individuals privately at a health club in Paramus, New Jersey, called Health Spa 2. That quickly grew to where I was training six to eight people a day for an hour session apiece. It quickly expanded, and I hired two people to work for me. It became a successful small company in a short period of time. During that time period, our first son, Sean, was born in 1990. The good thing about not necessarily being with the team anymore was I wasn't traveling as much, away from my family, or away from my wife during pregnancy. That was making a positive out of a negative.

From 1988 to 1993, I was continuously contacting teams and seeing if there was an opening in some capacity. One team that I almost got hired by was the Detroit Lions. I flew out to Michigan and met with them. The strength and conditioning coach that had been there, Gary Wade, was another friend of mine from Nebraska. It all goes back to that program's launching pad. Wade got hired directly from Nebraska by the Lions, but he was going to leave there to go back to college and take a job at Clemson. He recommended me to Detroit. I remember going up there, and Wayne Fontes was the head coach at the time. I met with him and their athletic trainers and I thought for sure as I was flying back that we were going to be moving to Detroit.

During the interview they were telling me not to cut myself short on the budget and to make sure to order two of everything because it's better to have too much than too little. The verbiage was all so positive that I thought I was getting hired. I did not.

Finally, in 1993 Jeff Torborg, whom I'd worked with on the Yankees, was the manager with the Mets and offered me a spot on his staff. I think it was a combination of me making contact and calling around and investigating and Torborg wanting to bring in someone familiar. I think the previous strength coach did somewhat of a roughshod job. It really soured the Mets on that position, and they were somewhat leery of bringing in someone at that time. They wanted someone to direct their program, but part of the stipulation was that I wouldn't travel with the team for the most part, which was somewhat of an issue regarding continuity of a program. Regardless, I finally was back with a major league outfit after a five-year absence. I soon learned there were as many memorable characters in Queens as there were in the Bronx.

DURING THE FIVE-YEAR HIATUS BETWEEN big league jobs, our family suffered a devastating loss. We didn't wait long after our son Sean was born in 1990 to have another child. Our daughter Shannon was born on Halloween of 1991. I remember thinking to myself that Halloween would never be the same after that. Three and a half months later, our lives were altered forever, as our healthy and beautiful baby suddenly passed away.

My wife Gale was employed at Pascack Valley High School as a guidance counselor and she was in a meeting after school on February 12, 1992. Our babysitter Nancy called frantically, and Gale's secretary barged into the meeting and said, "Gale, there is something wrong with your baby!"

Gale sped to the babysitter's home and made an emergency call to me at Health Spa 2 in Paramus and cried, "Jeff, something is wrong with our baby! Get here as soon as you can. Shannon's not breathing."

My heart raced, and I experienced a surge of panic as I jumped into the car and sped to what was at the time Pascack Valley Hospital in Westwood, New Jersey. I was actually hoping I'd get pulled over for speeding on the way there so the police could give me an escort to the hospital and I could get there as quickly as possible.

When I arrived, Gale was in the hospital room in anguish, just screaming and crying. The paramedics worked on reviving Shannon for about 45 minutes. Then the coroner pronounced her dead. We were all just in shock. Shannon had died from sudden infant death syndrome (SIDS). It was the most devastating experience you could imagine. Our son Sean was only 22 months old, and Shannon was just three months and twelve days old. Little was known about the syndrome at the time, but more recent research has identified some triggers that are like a domino effect with the simultaneous shutdown of the heart and respiratory systems.

We were led into a small private room. Our daughter's lifeless body was handed to Gale. She asked for a blanket because our baby was cold. Our priest from Most Blessed Sacrament arrived and gave Shannon the blessings and prayed with us. Father Carl was a godsend. He journeyed with us for the next two years, writing letters every day for weeks and then twice a month for the following years. He was deeply moved by our loss. Father Carl said it was one of the most profound moments of his priesthood.

When we arrived home, several of Gale's closest colleagues were in our small home to support us as we walked through the door without our daughter. Our baby appeared perfectly healthy and had just undergone her three-month checkup nine days before. We had been trying to put an addition on our two-bedroom home to create another bedroom for Shannon. We waited for the approval from the town for months with many delays, as the room we were adding was supposed to be finished before the birth of our child. We attended a town council meeting the night before, and it was announced that our addition was denied. We both were disheartened, and Gale didn't take it well and broke out in tears openly at the meeting. She cried most of the night before saying, "Jeff, I don't care if we have to live in a tent. We have our beautiful babies—Sean and Shannon. We will be okay."

Needless to say, we did not get much sleep that night. Gale nursed the baby at 3:00 AM and only slept a few hours before going to work at her school the first thing in the morning. There was nothing eventful about the morning except fatigue and disappointment. Later that morning Gale explained that Nancy, our babysitter, called and said she was available to bring the babies over to Gale's office to visit at 11:30 AM so she could introduce them to her staff. Her closest colleagues crowded in and out of her office at the school to hold the baby for about 45 minutes.

The strangest twist to the story is that Gale had a colleague, Kerry, who was her maternity leave replacement during her pregnancy with Sean. Kerry had lost her child to SIDS 15 months earlier. On our tragic day, Gale remembers Kerry holding Shannon in her arms and marveling at how beautiful she was. Gale said she was overwhelmed with survivor's guilt as Kerry had recently lost her only child. Gale started to feel some strange sensations while Kerry was holding Shannon and noticed that the baby's hands and feet looked bluish. During this brief visit, Shannon had sneezed and then vomited. After being held by several people, this wasn't unusual, but Gale discerned something didn't feel right. Gale asked Kerry if she was all right. They both attributed it to the frigid winter temperature. In hindsight now we know that it was a sign of poor oxygen, and something was happening to our daughter.

Three hours later Gale sped around the corner to the babysitter's house, which was only minutes away from the school. Twelve emergency vehicles were outside the home. Gale jumped out of her car and ran to the door. The sight will never leave her. Sean ran to her and grabbed her around the knees as she gasped in horror at our daughter, who laid lifeless on the coffee table as the paramedics tried to revive her. Gale pulled Sean into her arms and started to pray for God to revive our baby and make her breathe.

We had just joined the Most Blessed Sacrament congregation two weeks earlier and had requested to baptize our baby there. The baptism was scheduled for Sunday, February 16, and our family and friends were flying in for it. Shannon died that Wednesday on February 12, 1992. We held a wake on Valentine's Day followed by her funeral the next day. Our family and friends participated in a burial instead of a baptism. Gale insisted on going to the baptism mass that Sunday. The other babies were baptized, and it was an agonizing experience. The priest shared our story in the homily, and he didn't know we were there. When we got up to receive communion, Gale was holding Sean. She wanted to acknowledge a new mother who was holding her baby while she was holding Sean. He took his bottle and bopped this other baby on the head, making him cry. The whole church was watching, and it was another heartbreaking moment. Somehow, though Sean was not yet verbal, we think he knew his baby sister was gone.

Five weeks later, it was Easter, and we made a visit to the cemetery to Shannon's unmarked grave. We were having a private moment of grief as I held my wife. We did not hear anyone approach, but then a man was crying and kneeling at his child's grave. When he stood up, we looked at each other. He said, "How did your child die?"

"We don't know," Gale said. "She died of sudden infant death."

We asked him about his child. He had opened his garage and accidentally backed over his son with his truck. His son was only 22 months old, and his surviving baby daughter was three months old. Eerily, our surviving son Sean was 22 months old, and we had lost our three-month-old baby girl. In that moment, here we were as devastated as we could be and looked into the eyes of a man whose pain was so profound that I will never forget it. We both felt like we had been struck by lightning. It was from that moment forward that we knew our tragedy was life-changing, but we would somehow survive. This was not a chance happening. It definitely felt like one of those uncanny, unexplainable spiritual awakenings.

This traumatic event in our life catapulted us into a deeper understanding of the vulnerability and value of life, faith, and family. We were both changed from this experience. Many people suffer loss, and it either propels them toward faith or away from it. For Gale and I, we were launched into a challenging journey as a married couple and young family. While protecting and loving our son Sean, we yearned to have another child. After our loss we encountered a five-year period of secondary infertility that tested our resilience trying to have another child. Gale endured testing, blood tests twice a week, and a multitude of infertility drugs to conceive. During this period we utilized reproductive technology with 36 inseminations, a frozen embryo transfer, and two in-vitro fertilization (IVF) procedures. We did conceive on the second IVF procedure, and it appeared to be a multiple pregnancy. We had also concurrently begun international and domestic adoption proceedings.

We were overjoyed on the day we found out that Gale was pregnant from the IVF procedure. That evening we received a call from the Russian adoption agency telling us that we had been selected to adopt a Russian baby girl who was three-and-a-half months old. This was a strange twist when that was the exact age of the daughter we lost. And now Gale also was pregnant. We had to turn down the adoption as we had a high-risk pregnancy. One-and-a-half weeks later, Gale suffered a miscarriage. This felt cruel, and it was difficult to understand. At this point we were more aggressive with the adoption options and once again we were selected to be adoptive parents for two local pregnant teenagers. We met with them in a diner, and it was surreal.

Gale discerned something amiss and she called the mother of the teen to ensure that she was really ready to give her baby to us. The teen's mom started to cry and said she didn't know how she could give up her first grandchild. The baby was born the next day, and the family decided to keep it. Again, this was a heartache, but we both felt it was not meant to be. Through all of this, Gale was sure we would have another child either naturally or adopted. One more time we were selected as adoptive parents, and three weeks before the baby was due, the birth mother also changed her mind and kept the baby.

It had now been five difficult years of trying to have another baby or adopt. We started one more final IVF procedure, and Gale endured the 40 days of shots again, as this was our final procedure allowed within our insurance coverage. Through all of this Gale was a warrior. This was difficult for both of us. When she was fertile, she would have to fly to various ballparks and cities to join me on the road with the Yankees. They always did an ultrasound to be sure her eggs were ready to harvest. They aborted the procedure because it appeared that she had a large cyst on her ovary. This was very upsetting and discouraging as we would have to wait two months before trying again.

Two weeks later, I was preparing to leave for spring training on February 13, 1995. That weekend, we had sold our small home and moved into our new one. On Sunday before I left for the airport, my wife was acting strange during the move as she didn't feel well and wasn't her usual organized self. She left to go to the pharmacy and came home. A few minutes later, I heard Gale screaming and crying. I didn't know what was wrong. She started yelling, "I'm pregnant! I'm *pregnant!*"

After five long years, she had never had a home pregnancy kit as blood work always had to be drawn with the extensive infertility treatment. The cyst was actually the corpus luteum, and the egg had been released. Our beautiful daughter Jaime was on her way. Jaime was born September 21, 1995, and the joy was overwhelming. Sixteen months later our son Jesse was conceived without any treatment and born on February 10, 1997. We were blessed with completing our family and we are forever grateful.

While I returned to the Yankees in 1998 for my second tour with the organization, we worked through the grief together. As you can imagine, the healing takes a very long time. You don't ever get over the loss of a child. Later, a wise grief counselor said: "In the beginning grief carries you. In time you learn to carry the grief."

Gale's response to this hardship was to do what she knew how to do best: reach out to others who shared our grief. She started making connections and set up a bereavement group for local parents who had lost their babies. Our pastor allowed us to host the group in our church within months of Shannon's death. We participated for two years, hosting families and hiring a grief counselor named Charlie to guide us through the experience. At the time there was not a local SIDS organization or support group. The closest was in New Brunswick, New Jersey, nearly 60 miles away from our town.

Later that that year, we met Joel Hollander, the CEO of all-sports New York radio station WFAN at the time, and his wife Susan at a state gathering for SIDS parents. They suffered a loss that year of their daughter Carly to SIDS. Joel shared his plans to work with iconic radio host Don Imus of WFAN and Tomorrow's Children Fund to host a fund-raiser for SIDS. We supported this effort and volunteered for many years to share our story on the radio show. Over the next several years, the WFAN Radiothon raised enough money to add an entire wing to the Hackensack Medical Center and the Tomorrow's Children floor in the Don Imus Building.

After Shannon's death, Gale and I continued to work to raise funds and awareness for Sudden Infant Death Syndrome, including the donation we made after selling the infamous Mike Piazza bat from the 2000 World Series. George Steinbrenner also helped out, typically doing things behind the scenes that sometimes don't get any acclaim or notice. He made a generous donation one year in Shannon's name during Imus' annual Radiothon on WFAN in conjunction with the CJ Foundation for SIDS.

Gale appeared on Imus' program quite often in her work with that organization, and Steinbrenner heard about it and donated

$5,000 to the foundation. Enough funds were raised through the Radiothon to build the Don Imus Ranch in Albuquerque, New Mexico. The Yankees' wives also held a benefit every year and in two of the years they supported Sudden Infant Death and Tomorrow's Children with the funds they raised at Mickey Mantle's restaurant.

Our son Sean was among a group of 11 surviving siblings of SIDS who were invited to the ranch for the first time for a 10-day dude ranch experience. I was driving over the George Washington Bridge to Yankee Stadium one morning when I heard Imus sharing stories about the kids at the ranch. He said, "Yeah, Fred just called me and told me young Sean Mangold was just bucked off of the back of a horse."

He was fine, but I about lost control of my car. They were talking about my son on the radio!

I HAD PROPOSED TO GALE—WHOM I'd met at the University of Florida—on December 30, 1983 at our team hotel in Jacksonville on the morning of Florida's appearance in the Gator Bowl against Iowa. I'd just been offered the job with the Yankees and I knew it was time to take the plunge. We were set to be married on July 9, 1984 during the All-Star break of my first year with the Yankees.

I'm a guy who does not like to miss work or to ask for days off, especially when it was my first year with the Yankees and in Major League Baseball. I delayed asking Yogi Berra, our manager, but we decided I needed one day off prior to the All-Star break and one day after the break in order to go down to Jacksonville, Florida, to get married. Gale's family is from Miramar, Florida, right outside of Fort Lauderdale. A very good friend of hers, Greg Fey, was a Catholic priest and was head of a church right outside of Jacksonville in St. Augustine. She wanted to get married by Greg, so that's where we held the ceremony. There's not much time to do it during the season, but we pulled that off.

We had made the full-time move that winter from Gainesville, Florida, to Ridgefield Park, New Jersey, about 15 minutes from Yankee Stadium. Frank Messer, the longtime Yankees announcer, lived in the same little town about three blocks away. My wife asked me one day if I'd officially asked Yogi for those days off for the wedding. I hadn't, and she started getting all over me about it. Finally, it got to the point when I knew I had to put in the request. I went into Yogi's office at Yankee Stadium, and I was so nervous and anxious. I told him I was getting married on July 9 and asked if I could have off one day before the break. After stretching the team and doing our pregame conditioning, my plan was to leave from Minnesota, where we were playing the Twins. I'd go to the airport and fly from there back to Florida. I dreaded that he was going to dress me down. I didn't know what to expect. But all he said was about five or six words in typical Yogi speak: "Okay, kid, no problem. Okay, kid."

I was so relieved getting the go-ahead from Yogi. I wasn't going to argue with him. So I just said thanks and walked out of the room. It was a night game on July 7. So I was stretching the team around 4:30 PM out on the field at the Hubert H. Humphrey Metrodome. I was going to leave right after that.

I called a cab to get to the airport in time, but I could not get out of Minneapolis that night due to severe storms in Florida. There were no planes going down there. I ended up going back to the game, went to my locker, got changed, and headed to the dugout around the third or fourth inning. Everyone was looking at me, asking me if I'd changed my mind, razzing me about getting cold feet. I eventually got to Florida the next day, and it's been 37 years we've been married as of 2021.

When it came to families, Steinbrenner could be very generous and considerate—even after initially doing the wrong thing. Arthur Richman was a former newspaper man who worked for the Mets for years and later was a close advisor to him. Steinbrenner had made a ruling one year that the support staff no longer would be given tickets to games for their families. My wife and our three kids had been going to almost every home game. We couldn't afford to buy those tickets, and neither could the other families in our position.

My wife drafted a letter to Steinbrenner, saying how she worked all day as a guidance counselor at a local high school and then would come home to grab our kids and go to Yankee Stadium. Gale explained how it was such a big part of our lives to support the Yankees and our family. It also gave us valuable time to be together, and for him to take away these tickets was just inconceivable and it put us in a financial bind. We hoped that he'd see her reasoning. My wife can be a real son of a gun, very determined, and I told her, "Okay, I'll get this letter to George."

This was my second stint with the Yankees. We were in Detroit to play the Tigers, and I was coming off the field after batting practice. The sun was going down and coming through at Tiger Stadium, and Richman was sitting behind the dugout two rows up with Steinbrenner.

I'm thinking to myself, *Shit, this is the time. George is right here.*

I went into the clubhouse, into my locker, into my satchel bag, and pulled out an envelope with Gale's letter inside. I went back outside and I reached over the dugout and said, "This is for George. Arthur, take this." I handed it to him and I remember walking back into the clubhouse thinking, *I'm done, I might be fired right here on the spot. This might be my last major league game.*

Around the third inning, word came down. I think it was one of the clubhouse guys from the visiting locker room. Someone wanted to talk to me. I went back to the clubhouse, and Richman handed me back the letter. It read: "Starting immediately, the change in the ticket policy will revert to what it previously was for our support staff." It was signed GMS, George M. Steinbrenner.

I thought, *Wow, my wife just stood down The Boss.* I was just the middleman, the messenger. It definitely was a pretty gutsy thing to do, and I carried that letter in my satchel for about 15 years. She was standing up for the batting practice pitchers like Mike Borzello and Charlie Wonsowicz, the interpreters, the bullpen guys. It might have been a risky thing to do, but she was standing up for everybody, and I think Steinbrenner appreciated that. That's Gale. She's always been a fighter for her family.

Meet the Mets

I WAS THRILLED TO BE BACK IN BASEBALL WHEN THE NEW YORK METS came calling in 1993, even though the Mets never registered a winning season during my four years in Queens. I did encounter some interesting characters and hilarious memories as I bided my time before returning to the New York Yankees for the start of three straight World Series championships in 1998.

It certainly was nice to be reunited briefly with manager Jeff Torborg, one of the coaches from my Yankees days. He didn't make it through May in what spiraled into a disastrous 59–103 season for what was dubbed by the press as "the worst team money can buy." What happened off the field that first year in Queens might have been even more embarrassing, including Bobby Bonilla physically threatening a reporter, Bret Saberhagen shooting bleach at other media members, and Vince Coleman throwing a firecracker out of a car window near a group of fans.

Torborg was replaced after only 38 games by Dallas Green, who had taken over as Yankees manager just as I was leaving the Bronx. Green and I got along well, and he definitely was from the old school. He commanded attention. He was physically imposing with a booming voice and a dominant personality. He was confrontational and not afraid to get in someone's face. He told me, "Run these guys hard, especially the pitchers."

The weird thing about a team that bad was that the pitching staff actually had some big names and plenty of talent. Dwight Gooden obviously had been a superstar in the 1980s, and I later worked alongside him with the Yankees, too. He made 29 starts that first year, but he ended up getting suspended again in 1994 due to cocaine use. Doc actually worked really hard. He wanted to get back to where he was after wasting some of that God-given talent. Between his starts he always worked hard with me. It was the power of drugs—not a lack of effort on his part—that brought his time with the Mets to an end.

I never saw anyone sweat the way he did. During the games he pitched, they'd have four or five jerseys and undershirts of his hanging there in the runway leading to the dugout so he could change every inning or so. His hat would just be drenched. As a strength and conditioning coach, I let players open up to me on a personal problem or with their lifestyle. I think that Doc was at least trying to utilize exercise to maybe burn away some of the problems and pent-up energy, but he got derailed again.

One hard-luck pitcher from those teams was Anthony Young. He was a good pitcher who's mostly remembered for a long 27-game losing streak over a two-year span in 1992–93. One day during his skid, I was in the weight room at Shea Stadium. The food room was right across from the weight room, and there was this little hallway that goes down underneath the stands. I peered out of the weight room to see what was going on and saw Young doing something odd. He had a note in his hand that had come in an envelope. He was reading instructions while kneeling down and had a book of long matches with him. It was a letter from a fan that told him if you take this book of matches, stack them together, lean them up in a teepee fashion, and light them on fire, it will take away your bad luck. He was trying to do it out of the way, where no one saw him do it. He looked at me, and I said, "Go for it, maybe it will help you." I wasn't going to try to stop him. I guess when you're in a slump you will try anything.

Bret Saberhagen had won two Cy Young Awards earlier in his career with the Kansas City Royals. He was a pleasure to watch pitch, even though he had some arm issues after he came over from the Royals. Shooting bleach at media members was a dumb decision, but he and John Franco were the characters on those teams who came up with pranks all the time.

I know Bonilla isn't remembered fondly by fans or the media for his time with the Mets, and they get mocked to this day because he's still getting paid by the team because of deferrals in his contract. He and reporter Bob Klapisch also nearly came to blows in '93, and Bonilla infamously told Klap he'd "Show him the Bronx."

Personally, though, it meant a lot to me that Bonilla took to my son Sean right away, whenever he'd be with me at the ballpark. He gave my son a glove with the No. 25 on it when Sean was very young. I guess that was one of the perks of having a father working in the major leagues. Todd Hundley also gave Sean different pieces of equipment. Whenever I'd see Bonilla later in my career, he'd always ask me, "How's your boy doing?" He treated Sean so well. Another time he gave him his sweatbands.

I feel like I saw a different side of him from the guy whose history with the New York media wasn't great, even though we actually got off to a rough start, too. Bonilla got there the year before me in 1992. Early in spring training of '93, the players came out with me to start practice in the morning, and Bonilla was late one day for the stretch. It wasn't the first time.

I'd let it slide once, but the second time, everybody else was out on the field, and then Bonilla just kind of sauntered out there with that little stride of his and in no hurry at all. I called him out because it had to be done. He was like, "Come on. It's only a couple of minutes. It's not going to hurt anything."

I said, "Bobby, we're a team. These guys are out here, and you need to be out here, too."

"Don't call me out in front of everybody," he shot back.

I told him, "You called yourself out by coming out here late."

We kept jawing at each other a little bit, but I wanted to show just because you're our big All-Star that I wasn't going to back down from you or treat you differently. By that interaction of me standing up to him, I think he and other guys respected that. His thoughtful interactions with my son came after that. We had a little spat, but that was it. I think it's true with all the players that they want to know what the rules are and know they are going to be abided by. They don't want anyone treated differently just because of the money they were were making.

Another Mets player who could be ornery during that time period was Jeff Kent, who came from the Toronto Blue Jays with outfielder Ryan Thompson in the trade for David Cone.

You could tell right away that Kent had a lot of pop in his bat even if I don't think anyone foresaw the career he ended up having after leaving the Mets. He had opposite-field power and he played very hard. He was maybe not the easiest guy to get along with or the friendliest guy. He was another one of those guys where New York wasn't for him. I don't think he liked it, especially with all the media there. He went on to have some career with the San Francisco Giants and Houston Astros. There aren't many second basemen who have his career numbers—377 home runs and at least 100 RBIs in eight out of nine years.

On one West Coast trip in San Francisco, I happened to be in Green's office on the visiting team's side at Candlestick Park. Green knew Willie Mays from years earlier, and wouldn't you know it? In walks the Say Hey Kid himself. It was unbelievable to meet him, and I think one of the main reasons that Green brought him in was to talk to Thompson, who had a world of natural talent and some decent power. They called Thompson into the office, and I was sitting there, and Mays said to Thompson that he'd heard a lot about him, that he had a lot of talent and a lot of potential. "How many home runs you got, son?" Mays asked.

I think Green was thinking that Thompson was swinging for the fences too much, and Thompson replied, "I've got three so far."

Mays then asked him how many he thought he could hit, and Thompson said, "About 30, 35."

"Well, son, you better get it going then," Mays said.

Very subtle. Thompson's eyes got real big. It was a funny moment. I think Green thought Thompson needed to be put in his place a bit. He was a very cocky kid. He never really did put it all together. Thompson actually briefly came to the Yankees when I was there in 2000. He was the one who hit the screaming line drive that hit Boston Red Sox pitcher Bryce Florie right in the eye. I remember being in the dugout, and oh, what an awful sound it was. As soon as it happened, I got up and walked to the clubhouse because I didn't want to see what transpired.

Some of the pranks that Franco and a few others pulled got us through those losing seasons. It was mainly Franco who was the ringleader of the group. Jay Horwitz, the Mets' longtime public relations director and one of the great characters in baseball, tells a story in his book, *Mr. Met*, which I actually saw transpire. He was like the Godfather with the Mets.

It was in my first spring training with the Mets in '93 in Port St. Lucie, Florida. The players took Horwitz out to one of the back fields and duct taped him down on an athletic trainers' table they'd brought out there. They tied him down and put bread crumbs on him for the birds to come in and pick at him. They turned the water sprinklers on, too. The way Horwitz is, he'd play along with everything. He was so beloved by everybody and knowledgeable about the franchise. This was one of my first Mets memories, and Horwitz just shrugged it off and went about his job.

Franco was the maestro of all the pranks. In 1994 talk show host Jay Leno, a constant critic of the Mets in his monologues, was at Shea Stadium to tape a segment for *The Tonight Show*. Some guys tried the three-man lift prank. Whenever they got a celebrity in the clubhouse or an athlete from another sport, they would try to convince them that Franco could lift all three guys at one time. This is done by having the person lay down on the floor, which is what we got Leno to do, and then have two guys on either side of him hook arms. The other guys usually were clubhouse attendants, and most of the time they're not the leanest individuals around. They're typically pretty rotund fellas. We're talking about close to 600 pounds between them, and Franco said he could lift all three of them up off the floor. They'd put a belt around the guy in the middle (in this case Leno) for Franco to grab ahold of. Leno agreed to do it, and they started to put some money in to wager on it. Franco then called out, "Where's Mangold? Get Mangold. I've gotta get warmed up."

I went there and tried to psych up Franco. I then got a weight belt from the weight room and said, "Johnny, you've got to wear this belt now." He stretched out and got loose, and they started to count down from three. When it got to one, about eight or 10 guys that in the locker room came in with mustard, mayonnaise, mixtures of ketchup, milk, juice, and whatever you else you can name. They threw all that on the guy that's getting pranked. Leno actually reacted well to it and clowned around with the guys. It was kind of strange in a way, and I think he might have been tipped off about it. He started laughing, and everybody was cracking up, but he went over by the shower room and had a change of clothes hanging there as if he knew something was going to go down. Regardless, it was great. It was good for team morale to laugh.

Another celebrity sighting when I was with the Mets was Tom Selleck. He was a good baseball player who was in the movie *Mr. Baseball* in 1992, where he played an American playing professionally in Japan. He took batting practice with us and did really well. I think he even hit a couple out of the park. Selleck looked like he had a nice swing, and you can't really fake that. When he played Babe Ruth, John Goodman looked like he'd never swung a bat before. You could tell Selleck was an athlete.

This incident took place at Shea Stadium, but here's what made it weird. I usually tried to come in right at the end of batting practice to shower before getting ready for the game. It was kind of odd that here was me and Selleck in the showers at the same time. There was nobody else around. We had some chitchat, but it was one of those strange things. Only in this job in the world of professional baseball would you end up in the showers with Selleck or watch Leno get doused with ketchup and mustard.

Another moment I won't soon forget was when Cliff Floyd, then with the Montreal Expos, broke his wrist in a game at Shea in 1995. Floyd was playing first base, Todd Hundley was at the plate, and on a slow roller to third, Floyd got pulled off the bag on a throw into the base line and broke his wrist applying the tag. Floyd was normally an outfielder, and a more experienced first baseman probably would have shifted across the bag into foul territory to catch the ball, but I'll never forget Floyd's awful scream. He was screaming like crazy. The x-ray room was in the back of our weight room, and I knew they'd be coming in there immediately afterward. I was in the weight room, and he was just in such pain. He shattered his wrist in like six places. It was really horrible.

Tim Bogar is also worth mentioning. He was a utility guy when I was there, a plug-in player. But you just knew that he was very savvy. He watched everything and was a step ahead of everybody else in terms of preparation and understanding situations. He managed briefly with the Texas Rangers in 2014 and then five years later he was the third-base coach of the Washington Nationals when they won their first World Series in 2019. I always knew he'd make a really good coach or manager if he decided to pursue that path.

Bogar was a member of what we'd call the bomb squad, guys on the bench who around the sixth inning of games would go into the weight room and stretch or get warm in case they had to go into the game as a pinch-hitter, pinch-runner, or defensive replacement. Bogar was always there, always ready, always sharp. He actually interviewed for the Mets' managerial opening in 2020, and I was hoping he'd get it, but they went in another direction.

Speaking of Mets managers, Bobby Valentine was brought in when Green was fired toward the tail end of 1996. I don't know if he had some other philosophies on training or wanted to clean house, but he made it known that he wanted to hire his own people. I was called into assistant general manager Steve Phillips' office and I immediately had bad vibes.

He said, "Jeff, we are making a change due to philosophical differences. We're not going to rehire you. We're going to let you go." He just left it at that and didn't cite anything specific. I was called into assistant manager Steve Phillips' office. After meeting with Phillips, I went to the weight room to pack my belongings from my locker. Valentine was there at the same time, but we never exchanged a single word.

They had their minds made up. It's a business. I've been fired or not rehired a few times, and these things happen. The toughest part was that Sean must've been six years old, and our childcare person was not available that day. My wife was working so I had to take Sean with me to Shea Stadium. He wasn't feeling well, and equipment manager Charlie Samuels let him lay down on one of the clubhouse couches while I met with Phillips. I just got fired and I've got a sick son laying there. We had to walk out to the car with all my stuff, and I remember driving back over the Triboro Bridge to head back toward New Jersey. It was just one of those head-shaking things, for sure. But I've always felt those type of days only make you stronger.

114 Wins

A YEAR AFTER I'D LEFT THE NEW YORK METS, NEW YORK YANKEES trainer Gene Monahan reached out to give me a heads up that I might be able to find my way back to the Bronx. The Yankees had won the World Series in 1996 in Joe Torre's first year as manager and then suffered a heartbreaking loss to the Cleveland Indians the following year in the American League Division Series. Monahan called me in January of 1998 and said, "Jeff, if you have interest in coming back, we might be making a change here, and your name is definitely one of the top names we're considering."

Bob Watson was stepping down as general manager just a few weeks before the start of spring training, and his assistant Brian Cashman was getting promoted. There were 11 different men—a couple with multiple tenures—to serve as GM under George Steinbrenner over his first 22 seasons, and then there'd be one (Cashman) over the next 22-plus years. "I'd really love to get you back in here and I'm just feeling out your interest," Monahan told me. "I can't say anything more at the moment, but if it's a go on your end, hang loose, and I'll get back to you as soon as I can."

A day or two later, Monahan got back to me and he wanted me to come to Yankee Stadium for a meeting. I met with Cashman briefly, but all of the negotiation and discussion of contracts and finances were with Monahan. Steinbrenner had given Monahan an allotment for a contract for me. I wasn't particularly happy with the offer and I was trying to get him to bump it up financially. "Jeff, I can't. You know how George is. He approved a number and said if you agree to that, that's fine. But if not, we'll move on and find somebody else," Monahan told me. "We want you and we'd like to have you. But there's no negotiation. This is how it is."

I ended up agreeing to the figure that was offered and I was just thrilled to have the chance to come back again and work with the Yankees, especially now that they were a team with a championship pedigree. What a year, what a ride, that entire 1998 season was from the day I arrived in spring training in Tampa, Florida, in February until I rode in my first championship parade down the Canyon of Heroes in Manhattan in October following a record-setting season for the franchise. During the year after I'd been let go by the Mets, I'd gone back to personal training and was working hard at that, but I was still continuing to knock on doors and contacting teams in various sports. Finally, something broke, and I was elated that it would be with the Yankees.

I flew down to Tampa as soon as possible to view the facilities. When I was with the Yankees in the '80s, they still were training in Fort Lauderdale. I had to meet some of the staff across the street at the minor league complex in Tampa. Steinbrenner's baseball people—such as vice president of player development Mark Newman—were there.

Obviously, this also would be my first exposure to Torre and his amazing coaching staff and to Derek Jeter and Mariano Rivera and all of the great players that comprised the core of what would become baseball's most recent dynasty. The first players I met were David "Boomer" Wells and David Cone. Right before the start of the season, I was looking to institute the use of these rubber stretching bands known as Jump/Stretch Resistance bands, which soon became very popular in the industry. They were very effective for the stretching of hamstrings, quads, glutes, lower back, etc. There were three different levels of thickness/tension to accommodate the needs of our players. We were working out at San Diego State University before our opener in Anaheim, California, and I was doing some one-on-one exercises with Wells and had him utilize one of these bands. I asked him what he thought of them, and he said, "Yeah, man, this feels really good. We have to keep using these."

I thought if Boomer liked working with these bands without complaining, everybody else was going to like using them. That's when we started having the whole team utilize them before games in the regular season. I'd been hired so close to the start of spring training that we couldn't get enough of them delivered quick enough for camp. It wasn't until the last couple of days that we received them.

Just for variety's sake and to prevent things from getting monotonous, I thought about not using bands before one game late in the season. Paul O'Neill asked where the bands were, and I told him not to worry about it, and that it was just a little change-up. O'Neill basically said, "The hell with that—I'm gonna go inside and get them. Where are they?"

He went inside by my locker area and grabbed the bag that held 25 to 30 of these stretching bands. He brought them out and started dispersing them around to everybody. Maybe there was a little superstition involved, but also it was about the way their bodies felt with the bands. O'Neill was all about routine and would do the same movements every time before games. Alex Rodriguez asked me multiple times about O'Neill's consistent workout routines before games. O'Neill was a creature of habit, and so many guys liked their routines to remain the same.

Players could be so superstitious. We were at Yankee Stadium before one postseason game, and instead of stretching the team by the batting cage, I decided to bring them out to the outfield. Again, it was just a way to change things up during a long year. We had won the night before, but I had the team go out to right field, and O'Neill and Chad Curtis voiced, "Wait a minute. We won yesterday. Why change anything?"

"Guys, we're better than luck," I said. "You might be superstitious, but you guys are better than luck. Let's go."

That kind of made them smile. Nobody had a problem with it. I definitely learned over the years that athletes were creatures of habit, but occasionally I tried to take them outside their comfort zones.

As remarkable as that season would be with an American League-record 114 wins, the first week on the West Coast made it look as if the season was going to fall apart before it started. For starters we nearly got into a harrowing bus accident, we had to have a team meeting in Seattle in the first week, and there even was talk in the papers of Steinbrenner firing Torre, coming off the division-series loss to Cleveland the previous October. Looking back, I definitely think how that season started made how it ended even more memorable.

Though we started the season in Anaheim, we flew out to the coast early to play two exhibition games in San Diego. The plane that we took out there landed in Tijuana, Mexico. It was this great big party plane, and I remember the crew telling us the Rolling Stones just had used it before we did. We boarded our buses in Tijuana after we landed, and one of the buses nearly tipped over after hitting a partition or a cement barrier in the street. The bus driver was taking a tight corner and he hit this concrete median, and the bus bounded the other way, even tilting on the right-side wheels. It came right back down to the ground after a couple of seconds, but that definitely shook everybody up.

One of my favorite souvenirs is the broken bat New York Mets catcher Mike Piazza threw at New York Yankees pitcher Roger Clemens.

Mike Piazza's broken bat from the 2000 World Series used to reside in my home office.

Mike Piazza argues with home-plate umpire Charlie Reliford after Roger Clemens threw the piece of a broken bat at him during the first inning of Game 2 of the Subway Series. (AP Images)

At the University of Florida in the early 1980s, I got to work with athletes like Neal Anderson, Wilber Marshall, Lomas Brown, and John L. Williams. It was there that I would draw the attention of George Steinbrenner.

From left to right: Dave Winfield, Don Mattingly, and Willie Randolph—three of my favorite guys from the 1980s—celebrate Mattingly's first-inning home against the Texas Rangers on May 17, 1985.

(AP Images)

I helped implement the first real strength program for the Yankees, and bench press was a staple exercise.

I worked as the strength coach of the New York Mets during the 1990s, becoming one of a handful of coaches who worked for both crosstown rivals.

I can attest that working for George Steinbrenner could be challenging, but no one did it with more finesse than the great Joe Torre. (AP Images)

Resistance bands became very popular among our players—especially Paul O'Neill—and I hold one at Dodger Stadium.

I lead Derek Jeter and Bernie Williams through their stretching routine during the late 1990s.

Trainer Gene Monahan and I celebrate in the locker room after winning the 1998 World Series against the San Diego Padres.

I attend the 2000 championship parade down the Canyon of Heroes with Paul O'Neill.

I hold the World Series championship trophy with Willie Randolph, who played for the New York Yankees from 1976 to 1988 and coached for them from 1994 to 2004.

It was an honor to meet president Bill Clinton and Hillary Clinton at the White House after we won the World Series in 1999.

My wife Gale and I share a moment with president George W. Bush at the White House after we won the World Series in 2000.

I stretch out Alex Rodriguez, who had an amazing work ethic but also came under scrutiny for his performance-enhancing drug usage.

My wife, Gale and our children, Sean, Jaime and Jesse - the greatest team ever assembled.
Our children spent many afternoons and nights at Yankee Stadium.

We lost two games in Anaheim right away and then a third straight in Oakland before finally getting our first win against the A's. We then lost our first game against the Mariners in Seattle to fall to 1–4. The Internet still wasn't as prominent and accessible back then, but family members and friends from back home were telling us about all the talk on the radio and in the papers that there already was some pressure being put on Torre by Steinbrenner. Cashman, who was just starting out as GM, was ordered back from the road trip and to report immediately to Tampa. It certainly felt like a reprimand or punishment for the slow start.

People say they don't read the papers, but everyone always had someone telling them what was going on. If there was word that Steinbrenner wasn't happy, I learned from my previous stint that there was always truth to that. We had gone out and added some significant players that winter, including All-Star second baseman Chuck Knoblauch from the Minnesota Twins in a trade and Chili Davis, a veteran designated hitter. We picked up Scotty Brosius from the Oakland A's to play third base and even Orlando "El Duque" Hernandez, who started the year in the minors after signing as a free agent out of Cuba.

We went to Seattle, and dropped the first game to the Mariners, who were managed by my old skipper Lou Piniella at that time. Piniella and O'Neill also had been together with the Cincinnati Reds and they had a frosty relationship the previous couple of years from on-field incidents between the Yankees and Seattle. Lefty Jamie Moyer threw at O'Neill in the first game of the series, and O'Neill and some other guys were pissed off that none of our pitchers retaliated. I learned right away what I'd already heard about Torre—that he always knew the right thing to say and the right time to say it in these situations—was correct. He held a team meeting before the game the next night, basically telling everyone, "We're better than this and we need to play like it. We're not taking it to anybody."

Torre didn't have many team meetings, but when he did, you always knew something was up, and he needed to get something off his chest. Cone stood up in that meeting and said, "Guys, we've got to stand up for each other."

O'Neill also stood up and said: "I'm tired of getting hit by these guys. This has got to stop. Hell, if we go up 10–0, let's go ahead and make it 15–0."

That night, we went out and took it to them right from the start. Knoblauch led off the game with a home run, Darryl Strawberry hit another homer, and we scored six times in the first inning for a 13–7 win. That meeting was a real awakening. It was so emotional. This was just a few games into my return to the team, and I already was thinking, *These guys are something special. We are going to kick some ass the rest of the way.*

Indeed, it didn't stop from that point on for the rest of the year. We just pounded teams day after day. That meeting and victory lit the fuse. We won eight in a row and 14 of 15 and never looked back the entire season. On the rare occasion we got beat, someone like Tino Martinez would walk around going, "The hell with this, let's go. Let's start another streak."

Nobody on that team was ever satisfied. The Yankees ran away with everything, finishing with 114 regular season wins and only 48 losses. We won the American League East by 22 games over the Boston Red Sox. I hadn't been there the year before, but so many of our guys said repeatedly how their loss in five games to Cleveland in 1997—especially after winning it all the year before against the Atlanta Braves—really stuck with them that entire offseason. Rivera was in his first season as closer, and he coughed up a costly home run to Sandy Alomar Jr. in Game 4 before the Indians sealed the series the following night. Bernie Williams said that losing in '97 was more of a lasting memory than the years that they won the World Series. It truly fueled them, and that 1998 team played with such a purpose and had such a professional attitude from top to bottom.

From Day One in spring training, I witnessed the focus, the professional approach, and the attention to detail. They worked on cutoffs, relays, and the essential basics that help you win games. It was truly special to watch. Beyond the stars like Jeter, O'Neill, Martinez, and Williams, that team had such an experienced bench. Davis got hurt and missed most of the summer, but guys like Strawberry, Tim Raines, Chad Curtis, and Luis Sojo provided such incredibly valuable professional depth. They'd plug in someone like Straw, and he could carry you for weeks at a time. By the end of the season, we brought up prospects Shane Spencer and Ricky Ledee who earned themselves playing time in October.

The veteran guys didn't ever complain. They knew their time would come and they stayed ready. I worked with all of those veteran players throughout that season, helping keep them ready for whenever their chance to play arose. They were savvy players and good teammates. Sojo was a conduit to the young Latin players like Ledee and pitcher Ramiro Mendoza, letting them know this was how we do it here. Torre set the tone and was perfect for this group of players. From that meeting in Seattle, these guys were just hellbent on winning every day. I'd never seen anything like it.

The starting pitchers just took the ball every day and did their jobs. They were workhorses. Andy Pettitte, Cone, Wells, and even Hideki Irabu and El Duque, who showed up in June and gave the rotation such a boost, were terrific. To front the bullpen, Rivera never let the crushing home run he'd given up in 1997 affect him. You'd never have known by talking to him or watching him go about his work that it even happened. The whole team had a winner's mentality.

The brawl against the Baltimore Orioles on May 19 two days after Wells had hurled his perfect game against the Twins showed that everyone supported each other. It truly had to be one of the wildest fights I've ever seen in baseball. Martinez got drilled in the back by Orioles closer Armando Benitez, and all hell broke loose. Relievers Jeff Nelson and Graeme Lloyd sprinted out of the bullpen and were throwing wild haymakers. Straw decked Benitez near the Orioles' dugout, and then the fight spilled down by their bench area. Strength and conditioning coaches and trainers aren't in uniform, so we were supposed to stay in the dugout during those melees. We were not allowed to take part in any on-field brawls. It was very tough not to join in, but I didn't go on the field that night. The next couple of days, Charlie Wonsowicz, who was our video coordinator, was breaking down videos with them and he slow-motion replayed all of it so we could see which guys on both sides were involved.

That was definitely a moment that people say brought us together. It was a hell of a few days. Boomer threw his perfect game on a Sunday against Minnesota, and then we had a scheduled off day. The Orioles came in on Tuesday, and it made for an unforgettable couple of games at Yankee Stadium. It really defined the spirit and togetherness of that team. The lasting memory for me was seeing Torre, Straw, and more of our guys ending up over there in Baltimore's dugout.

Right after the brawl happened, I remember an interaction as clear as day. I was in the runway in the tunnel, and O'Neill came to find Irabu, who was in the walkway, smoking a cigarette. O'Neill got right in his face and said, "You know what you have to do!"

Irabu just kind of threw his shoulder back and made this animal sound, this grunt, showing he understood. The next night Irabu drilled Mike Bordick and Brady Anderson of the Orioles and he left the mound to a standing ovation.

Later that season, probably the best thing Irabu ever did as a Yankees pitcher was when he was pitching for us in September against the Toronto Blue Jays. Roger Clemens was on the mound for the Blue Jays and he plunked Brosius with a pitch. The next inning Irabu drilled Shannon Stewart and then Irabu charged the hitter—not the other way around. The fastest I ever saw him run was when he charged from the mound to home plate to start a brawl. Most of the time when a pitcher hits someone on purpose, they'll stand there and wait for the batter. Not this time.

Torre really gave me free reign that year of what to do in terms of prepping these guys to play. He was savvy enough to delegate; at this point he was a maestro of being a player's manager. He'd let everybody do their thing, but if he saw something that was out of bounds, he wasn't going to hold back any comments. Torre worked out a lot, too. He worked out with me just about every day. It wasn't with the ulterior motive to be in the weight room and check up on guys. He just enjoyed it and knew he needed it for himself and his health. It also gave him the opportunity to see how I worked with people, how I gauged the guys, and how I communicated with them. He showed confidence in my abilities and how I handled the players.

Some guys were different. For example, El Duque had really unique training methods. It must have been what he'd learned in Cuba. I had this stopwatch, and he'd tell me to time him for two minutes and he would go around in circles really fast. It was like that hazing drill when you see someone holding a bat against the ground and they run around the bat as fast as they can to see how dizzy they can become. El Duque would do that for two minutes, but his equilibrium and his balance were simply phenomenal. He'd do this for two full minutes and then fight to balance himself, but he'd never fall over. It was astonishing. He'd also do these series of headstands up against a wall and do that for a minute at a time. His conditioning and running work were exceptional.

You know that high knee lift he would do in his delivery? I have a picture of him in the weight room where he's doing that leg kick while holding an Olympic bar with 45-pound plates on each side. That was 135 pounds on his upper back. He would do step-ups onto this box that was two-feet high to resemble his pitching motion. He would overload the technique over and over. By the time he'd go out on the mound, he'd have the muscular endurance and muscle memory to repeat this movement over and over again.

Training pitchers wasn't about cardiovascular efficiency or aerobic conditioning as much as it was about muscular endurance. The key is for your legs to consistently push off the mound and maintain the same stride length and landing spot and to not have your legs start to wobble or get fatigued. That way they can maintain arm slot and release location. As soon as the legs go, they're done and they start to lose control. That's why we tailored the workouts for pitchers to focus on their legs.

Speaking of guys with incredible endurance and obvious physical and mental toughness, people forget that in September of that year we were in Baltimore on a Sunday night when Cal Ripken Jr. came out of the lineup for the first time. It ended his streak of consecutive games at 2,632. For a guy to play that many games in a row is incredible, and it wowed me in particular since I was a strength and conditioning coach. He was a big man for a shortstop at the time—by then they had moved him to third base—at 6'4", probably 225 pounds, just being mentally and physically tough enough to handle never taking a day off is incredible.

I remember the first time I saw Ripken work out was in Baltimore. I don't recall what year it was. It was during my first stint with the Yankees in the 1980s. He was doing these very intense interval sprints on the Woodway Treadmill, the Mercedes-Benz of treadmills. It's German made, it's wider than normal ones, and the acceleration is immediate so there's no lag time. It promotes tremendous workouts. He was doing some really intense interval sprints on the Woodway. This was after a game. I was very impressed to see him going through this series of sprint intervals for 30-40 seconds at a time.

Ripken played through all those bumps, bruises, and strains, but his game never suffered from it, nor did his team. From a physical standpoint, to account for a guy not missing even one game for 15 years, it's just so special. I can't fathom it. It had to be all self-motivation, like he never needed a push. It takes a special man. Everybody, including his opponents, got up on the top step of our dugout and deservedly applauded him on September 20. We won that night like we usually did. We went on to win eight of our final nine games to finish with 114 victories, the most in franchise history and American League history. Piniella's Mariners would eclipse our mark with 116 wins in 2001, but we eliminated them in the playoffs that October. When you win that many games in the regular season, none of it matters if you don't win the World Series.

That was something we were about to find out in the ensuing weeks.

A Nice Ring to It

AFTER THE 1998 REGULAR SEASON THE NEW YORK YANKEES HAD JUST completed, we were starting to get almost a rock band following wherever we went—whether that was getting on and off the bus at the hotels or during batting practice. Even though the Yankees always had enjoyed a massive following anyway, this was special. This was different.

At the same time, it almost felt like during the regular season, even though we had a record-setting year, as if we were an afterthought in many ways. That's because that year really was all about the home run chase between Mark McGwire and Sammy Sosa in the National League. It was almost as if the playoffs marked the first time the media outside of New York was paying attention to the Yankees because of how we cruised through the 162-game slate. We had such a big lead in our division, and now all of a sudden it was like, okay, these 114 wins mean nothing if we don't seal the deal.

You could just feel the immediacy of things getting ratcheted up in Game 1 of the American League Division Series against the Texas Rangers. Getting off to a good start and getting things going in the right direction were paramount. Another thing I can't forget is that a day or so before the playoffs started, we found out that Darryl Strawberry was suffering from colon cancer. That really floored the team, but it also served as an unforeseen rallying cry. Several players were quite close to Straw. Chili Davis was from the same part of Los Angeles as Straw. Tim Raines also was really tight with him. A lot of the younger guys were, too. His teammates looked up to him for all he'd overcome in his life, namely the battles with drugs from earlier in his career with the New York Mets and the Los Angeles Dodgers. He'd also contributed monster offensive numbers to our lineup that year with 24 home runs and a .542 slugging percentage in only 295 at-bats. When we swept the Rangers in Arlington, Raines got the whole team together for a toast and said, "This is for Straw!"

That clinching Game 3 actually was rain-delayed for hours. It was like a monsoon. It absolutely poured. They had a state-of-the-art drainage system in Texas, though, so no matter how much it rained, the field would be fine, and it was. It was incredible. Eventually, David Cone pitched a gem, Shane Spencer and Paul O'Neill went deep, and I'll never forget the guys chanting "Dar-ryl, Dar-ryl" in the clubhouse afterward.

The Cleveland Indians were up next in the American League Championship Series, and it was a shot at redemption for our guys after losing to the Indians the previous fall. What a lineup they had with Manny Ramirez, Jim Thome, Kenny Lofton, David Justice, Travis Fryman, Sandy Alomar Jr., Omar Vizquel. You just knew that these guys could blow you out of the water at any time. Whenever you'd see Ramirez or Thome make an out, you were just relieved. It was a phenomenal offensive team.

The difference was our guys were one unit, a true team. The Yankees didn't care about numbers; they didn't care about the headlines. We just wanted to win and the other accolades would come with it. That was one thing I learned from that year more than anything. The important thing was just to be a team, to be a group, and to not worry about personal accomplishments. These guys knew the only accomplishment that counted, that mattered, was to be World Series champions.

Of course, it almost didn't happen. After taking the ALCS opener at home, our biggest fears were realized when we fell behind two games to one in the best-of-seven set. The ending of Game 2 in New York was an absolute disaster. We were in position to take a 2–0 series lead, but Chuck Knoblauch brain-locked on a bunt play in the top of the 12th inning. Covering first base he let the ball roll away while arguing with umpire John Shulock that he was interfered with by the runner, Fryman. That enabled Enrique Wilson to rumble and stumble around third base and score the go-ahead run before the Indians added two more for a 4–1 victory to even the series. Two days later, we got shut down by Indians right-hander Bartolo Colon and we were in trouble.

All of a sudden, those 114 wins and the sweep of Texas didn't mean much. This was before anybody really knew about what a postseason legend Orlando Hernandez was about to become. El Duque had been with us since June and performed phenomenally, going 12–4 with a 3.13 ERA over 21 starts. Still, nobody expected he was going to toss seven shutout innings in his first career postseason appearance in Game 4, leading us to a 4–0 win to save the season essentially.

Hernandez was just as good as he could be. With his off-speed pitches, his control, his focus, he was totally unfazed, and I think everybody fed off of his confidence. We didn't lose another game that October, finishing with seven wins in a row. Honestly, some guys were tight going into that Game 4. We had won all these games and all of a sudden we were pushed to the brink. It took a masterful performance by El Duque to pull us through. Obviously, personality-wise, he was not your typical rookie because of everything he went through in Cuba and getting to the United States. He was one of those guys who relished the big time, the bright lights, the primetime. He rose to the occasion. He loved the spotlight. Like Derek Jeter, they take it to another level when the moment is really important. Even after he left New York, El Duque had the numbers to back that up with a career ERA of 2.55 in 19 postseason games.

Also, our lineup that year would just wear down opposing starting pitchers. The batters would drive up that pitch count, and around the fifth or sixth inning, that starter would have to come out of the game. The Yankees would get him up to 100 to 110 pitches and then feast on a team's bullpen. We had great pitching too, but these guys would take pitches, would foul off pitches, would work the count full, and just had a way of wearing people down. It was an all-year thing, getting into opposing bullpens.

Knoblauch had his throwing issues at second base, but adding him to the top of that lineup that year really made a huge difference. The team kind of adopted his philosophy of battling and seeing so many pitches to set up the rest of the lineup. It was such a lineup of grinders, but also these guys put in the work with me and on their own. They worked hard in the weight room. When we went on the road, and the time would come to utilize the other team's facility, we would go in there in with a drove of players. I think that somewhat added to the intimidation factor of winning a lot of games and playing well. Other teams saw how hard we prepared and that these guys were strong.

Take someone like Homer Bush. He didn't play that much that year. He would pinch run mostly and get in the lineup occasionally, but you could see why he was a fan favorite. He was always smiling and had a great personality, but he was a weapon, too. He stole some key bases for us. What a weapon and luxury he was. A team like that, you tend to remember and think about all of the big names, but guys like Homer and Luis Sojo, Ramiro Mendoza, who could start or relieve, were so valuable and important to the success.

Scott Brosius came over from the Oakland A's and just had an unbelievable year, recording 98 RBIs while batting ninth for much of the season. I've never seen anyone who could come in on a ball at third base like Brosius. He'd barehand a slow roller and then complete it with a perfect throw to first. I don't know how many times he did it, but it never got old. He was just fabulous at that. He also obviously had a monster World Series. It's not often that the No. 9 hitter on a team like that becomes the MVP of the Fall Classic.

After we ousted Texas and then Cleveland, it was World Series time. To have the opportunity to play for a championship ring was becoming a reality. I never thought I'd get to that point after some of those early years with the Yankees, especially after being with the Mets and losing so many games.

In our meetings before the World Series, we were waiting to see who'd win the National League Championship Series between the San Diego Padres and Atlanta Braves. The hitters and pitchers were going about their respective meetings, and as they finished up, they slowly walked out to batting practice. Paul O'Neill was talking to Gene "Stick" Michael, the former Yankees general manager who still worked in the front office after helping acquire much of that roster. "Stick, just tell us, can anybody beat us? Any of these teams?" he asked.

"Nah, nobody can beat us," Stick replied.

"That's all we wanted to hear," O'Neill said.

We opened up in New York against the Padres, and in the first game, San Diego grabbed a 5–2 lead against David Wells, including a home run by outfielder Greg Vaughn. I thought all along these guys would play us tough because the Padres had Vaughn, future Hall of Famer Tony Gwynn, Kevin Brown as their ace, and Trevor Hoffman in the bullpen. That lead wouldn't last, as we put up seven runs in the seventh inning to take control of the game. Knoblauch tied it with a three-run blast, and then Tino Martinez crushed a full-count grand slam into the right-field seats to put us ahead. Bedlam ensued after that.

Everybody focuses on the location of the previous pitch by Padres lefty Mark Langston that was called a ball. He clearly thought it was strike three. It definitely looked like it could have been. Either way the place was absolutely rocking after Martinez's blast, and that just took it over the edge. The atmosphere might've been exceeded by the 2001 World Series after the 9/11 attacks, but Yankee Stadium was the craziest I'd ever experienced to date when Martinez went deep. It felt like the stadium was going up and down like an accordion.

I wasn't there in 1996 when Joe Girardi hit the big triple in the Game 6 clincher against the Braves, but I had never heard it that loud before that night of Game 1 in '98. The adrenaline was flowing from the first pitch, and things got so ratcheted up. It's so draining for the players to play 162 regular-season games and 25 spring training contests. You get to this point, and these guys are tired and fatigued, but the adrenaline from the crowd can take you to a point where your body can do things you didn't know it could. It's an unbelievable feeling.

For me as the strength coach, it still was business as usual, but I'd back the guys down and tell them, "Listen, I wouldn't worry too much about lifting right now. If you want to, if you feel good, if you feel fine and recuperated, go ahead and train."

I would try to make sure they could reduce the level of their work if they needed to, but a lot of that, too, comes down to superstition. Players are creatures of habit, so I would give them free reign of what they wanted to do. I wouldn't scold anybody or get on anybody because at that point I knew they were fatigued and I trusted that each guy knew what he needed to do personally to prepare. I was more focused on just preparing them before the game to get loose, to keep the blood flowing, to work up a sweat, and to get ready to go. I was just trying to get out of the way and let them go. It's kind of like a racehorse. You want to get that horse lathered up, but at that point, it's up to them. Just let them run. Another analogy is that of a boxer. If you see a boxer come into the ring and he's not sweating, there's a problem.

After another win in Game 2, the Yankees headed out to San Diego with a 2–0 lead, and the confidence level was sky high while flying out there. Our guys knew we were the better team and the best team. We knew that we should win and we expected to do so. Losing is always a possibility. That's why you play the games, of course, but their confidence was growing.

Before our first game out there, I went out running. Instead of doing so in the stadium, I ran out and around the parking lot area. Everybody was tailgating, but I sometimes liked to get a feel for the stadium and for the area. I remember all these people grilling, drinking, and getting ready for Game 3. As I ran through there, I was saying to myself, *Folks, you're going to be sad. You're in for a letdown because we are going to beat you tonight.*

The moment was very special and memorable. During the playing of the national anthem before our first game in San Diego, the only Yankees along the left-field line completing warmups were Bernie Williams and myself. They played the anthem and they had a huge flag out across the outfield with probably about 80 to 100 people holding it. It got to the point that the flag got up off the ground pretty high. Right toward the end of the anthem, Williams took off running toward left center and kind of disappeared underneath the flag. The crowd was going crazy, and nobody else saw him, but I saw him. It was Bernie being Bernie underneath the flag in left-center field. That was pretty funny.

We were losing 3–0 in the seventh inning in Game 3 before Brosius got our offense started with a leadoff home run against former Yankees lefty Sterling Hitchcock. We were still down 3–2 in the eighth when the Padres summoned Hoffman, their Hall of Fame closer. (As of 2021 he was second all time in baseball history behind Mariano Rivera in career saves.) They were blaring his entrance song, AC/DC's "Hells Bells," and about 60,000 people were waving their white towels for him to escape the jam. Of course, Brosius then took him to dead center for a three-run homer and a 5–3 lead, and that just about took out whatever air was left in San Diego's balloon, that's for sure. I actually think our guys were excited to see Hoffman. They wanted to face him, they wanted to get him. The attitude was: bring us your best, give us your best guy, and we're gonna get him. Brosius got him.

Brosius, the MVP of the World Series, drove in another run the next night, Andy Pettitte carried a shutout into the eighth, and Rivera locked it down in the ninth to complete the sweep. To finally win the World Series, the jubilation and satisfaction you feel and the culmination of all that work and time put in was just an indescribable feeling.

Once we got to the latter innings of Game 4, everybody just kind of started looking at each other, and things started speeding up in my mind. You start to realize this might be real. And then there's another out and you get even closer. I was watching Pettitte, ever focused, not showing any emotion. And then we brought in Rivera for the ninth inning. Everybody was crowding around each other on the bench because you didn't want to miss anything. You tried to take it all in, and everybody's looking at each other and elbowing each other like, "Wow, here we go."

You try to keep calm. It was not over yet, but when it came to the point that Rivera got the ground ball to third, and Brosius zipped it over to Martinez, I was just ecstatic, almost in shock. It's pretty obvious to say it was a great feeling. To realize you're the last team standing, that you accomplished what these guys wanted to be from Day One, and to get to the point you're the last one on the hill was astounding. The visiting locker room was small, but the champagne was flowing, and we were all getting doused. What a feeling it was to taste the champagne for the first time and have it drip over my face.

At some point we found out that we were going to stay the night, and the Yankees arranged for us to have dinner at San Diego Chargers linebacker Junior Seau's restaurant. Jim Leyritz, the former Yankees catcher and 1996 World Series hero who was on the Padres that year, actually arranged it. Leyritz has said that George Steinbrenner asked him where they could go out in San Diego that night, and The King arranged for us to hang out at Seau's.

My wife Gale was out there with me, too, and I called my father in Iowa the next day to share that experience with him. I later gave him the World Series jacket that I had been given. He loved it and wore it and showed it off all around Sioux City, Iowa.

They say you never forget your first, and it's so true. I have my first World Series ring in a safe at home and I remember the excitement of Ring Day the next year. To have your name called by Bob Sheppard and to go up to home plate at Yankee Stadium to receive it from Brian Cashman is special. I remember I got the box and immediately went inside to my locker. It was beautiful, not gaudy. Some rings like that are very gaudy, and I loved that they put our 1998 record for the regular season and playoffs—125–50—on one of the sides.

The championship parade also was my first, and Gale and my eight-year-old son Sean got to experience that with me. The bus ride went down to Battery Park, where we boarded the floats. People, who'd been through it before, told me that I might want to consider having the family wear ear plugs because it gets so loud riding down the Canyon of Heroes. I thought, *Are you kidding me? I can't do that. I want to hear everything.*

Of course, as soon as we began making our way along the parade route, the echo and reverberation of sound from probably two million people was deafening. When we came to an intersection, the cross streets there were jammed two blocks down in each direction. The whole street was overflowing with people 10 or 20 deep. People hung out of windows of their office buildings. It was more people than the entire population of the town I grew up in, that's for sure, and the onlookers were all within a mile or so. There was constant noise, and people tried to get to your float and catch a glimpse of the Yankees.

There's a picture I have coming up Broadway of all the floats. I can see where we are. There are toilet paper rolls coming down that didn't unfurl. Up on the ledge of one of the office buildings probably about seven or eight stories high, there was this woman out on the ledge completely naked. I looked up there, and she's jumping around. Sean saw it and started laughing and pointing. It was a party, and we were celebrating.

Finishing up at City Hall, we all received our keys to the city from Mayor Giuliani. Little did I know that wouldn't be my last ring, my last parade, nor my last key to New York City. Because once you get a taste of winning, all you want is more.

12

Perfection

WHEN I FIRST ARRIVED IN TAMPA, FLORIDA, IN 1998 TO BEGIN MY second stint with the New York Yankees, the first two players I ran into happened to throw perfect games in successive seasons. One of the first times I was in the trainer's room at the minor league complex, David Wells and David Cone were in there working out. I introduced myself as the new strength and conditioning coach, and one of the first things Boomer ever said to me was, "You know, I'm kind of heavy, but I pitch better when I'm heavy."

I shot back kiddingly, "Well, it looks like you're getting ready to have quite a year then."

I think they saw right away that I could dish it out as much as I could take any ribbing.

Players enjoy that. They never want to work with somebody who is very touchy or oversensitive, who takes things too seriously. I don't do that and I know how these guys are. They have to have fun and let off some steam sometimes. That's part of it, and if they have to do it at your expense occasionally, that's part of the deal.

We all know that Boomer went on to have a monster year in 1998, winning 18 games and throwing his perfect game against the Minnesota Twins on May 17. Having a guy like Wells, who didn't take strength and conditioning too seriously, that was part of the challenge of the job.

Boomer also was an extremely agile guy for someone his size. He was heavy, but he was a much better athlete than people gave him credit for. He had good feet, good coordination, and good balance.

For anybody to have the delivery that he had and to be able to repeat that delivery so often throughout a game, which is maybe the most important thing for a pitcher, is very impressive. To be able to duplicate that movement and muscle memory, to have your arm in the correct slot and a certain stride length, you couldn't do that unless you're physically gifted. Make no mistake, Wells was a horse. He was heavy, but he had a muscular frame. He wouldn't go the extra mile, you might say, or put in any extra time to improve himself physically. He'd go in spurts where he wouldn't work out for a while, and then I'd go and talk to him, and say, "Come on, Boomer, let's go and make some changes starting with your next start. Let's get some work in, some consistency."

Two starts before the perfect game, Joe Torre actually had called Boomer out publicly in the media for being out of shape. We were in Texas, it was like 100 degrees, we had a big early lead, and Wells couldn't get through the third inning. He gave up seven runs, but we won the game by a high score 15–13. There wasn't any conversation directly from Torre to me about getting Wells into better shape. Maybe some things are better left unsaid, and the staff just knew that everybody had to be a bit tougher and more focused on him. That definitely might have been one of the moments where I pulled him aside and said we had to do something to see if we could get some consistency and get going again.

I do remember that night in Texas as a low point, and then two starts later, he went out and threw his perfecto. It really was unfathomable. I sat in the same place on the bench the whole game over by where Coney was sitting. I was on the other side of Torre and Don Zimmer but not all the way down toward the far end where the water cooler was located. Each time Boomer would record the third out of an inning, I would get up and move around. He was coming over to sit near Coney, one of the only guys who would break the protocol or superstition of not talking to a pitcher throwing a no-hitter.

I would get up and walk over to the bat rack area, and Boomer first would come in and knock the dirt off his cleats up against the wall. While all of this was going on, I was thinking, *Here he goes again.* He might not have been super serious about the conditioning aspect of things, but he knew his Yankees history and he was a superstitious guy. He did that each inning. That's what I remember most about it.

As the drama was building, it was one of the most magical moments ever at Yankee Stadium, certainly in the years when I was there. After we completed the fifth or sixth inning, it felt like just the emotion and the power of Yankee Stadium and the fans were going to pull him through it. You could feel that extra oomph, the extra adrenaline in the stadium that day. It made the hair on the back of your neck stand up. The electricity was off the charts. Coney said to him in the latter innings, "Hey Boomer, show me something: break out that knuckleball."

And Boomer let out a big laugh. Coney has said he thought that let Boomer exhale just a little. He had to be feeling the pressure. I know Wells has said often how nervous and anxious he was. Despite his tough guy persona and him saying that he was hungover from the night before, Boomer cared about baseball history and Yankees history. He also attended the same high school that 1956 World Series perfect game author Don Larsen attended in the San Diego area. Boomer definitely knew what a big deal that was as the game unfolded.

People always talk about a key defensive play that saves the pitcher in those situations. For Wells that came in the eighth inning with Chuck Knoblauch's play at second base. Knoblauch had those throwing yips going on, and there was a hot smash right at him that he knocked down with a backhand stab. Everybody held their breath, but Knobby fired a dart over to Tino Martinez at first. He didn't have time to even think about it. We knew right then that there was a good chance Wells was going to get it, and you could see his excitement and relief when Paul O'Neill secured the final out on a fly ball to right field by Pat Meares.

Boomer certainly made the most of that instant celebrity, and winning the World Series later that year only made the feat stand out so much more. It also made Wells' inclusion in the blockbuster trade for Roger Clemens the following spring that much more devastating for him.

Wells was like a hero around town, a folk hero really, and then right at the beginning of spring training when we'd only been there a few days, he was sent off to the Toronto Blue Jays with Graeme Lloyd and Homer Bush for Clemens, who'd won the fourth and fifth of seven career Cy Young Awards the previous two seasons.

We were all shocked, but for me this was the confirmation of how the Yankees operated, especially under George Steinbrenner: never be complacent, always try to do whatever possible to improve, even though we'd won it all in runaway fashion the previous year. Even after the magic in 1998, Steinbrenner and Brian Cashman were trying to get even better. I think they saw this opportunity to get Clemens and weighed the factor that this was the best they were going to get out of Boomer in New York—as if he'd maybe reached his zenith, and they were unsure if he could continue going at that level of performance. His value certainly was never going to be higher than it was after '98. The trade maybe added to the pressure to repeat in 1999 while also telling everyone it's a new year and something a little different. The expectations didn't change. The organization was looking at it as definitely being a positive, the rare opportunity to bring in Clemens, one of the greatest pitchers in baseball history.

Another major decision Steinbrenner made during that offseason was his long overdue reconciliation with Yogi Berra, who had stayed away from Yankee Stadium for 14 years after Steinbrenner fired him 16 games into the 1985 season. Yogi made his grand return at the home opener in '99 and then he came back again—along with his 1956 World Series perfect game battery mate, Larsen—on July 18 for Yogi Berra Day. Unfathomably, with that as the backdrop, Cone forever joined Larsen and Wells that afternoon as the only three pitchers in Yankees history to author a perfect game. It was truly astonishing.

It was just a hot, humid day, a real scorcher on a Sunday afternoon against the Montreal Expos. You could tell the game wasn't going to go on uninterrupted for very long because it was supposed to storm like crazy. Then the skies opened up in the third, delaying the game for 33 minutes. After the first inning when Coney came off the mound, he was beet red, sweating like crazy. The veins in his neck were popping out, and I remember thinking, *Man, this is going to be a long day for him.*

If that rain delay had gone on any longer, Torre has said that he wasn't going to send him back out there. Coney obviously had dealt with different shoulder issues, including an aneurysm in 1996, and the rain probably lasted just short enough for him to come back and continue that day. With his medical history, especially the aneurysm and being an older guy at 36, he had a lot of mileage on him.

Cone's perfect game created just an unbelievable feeling, another example of the kind of experience that raises the hair on your neck. It was all from the crowd. You wouldn't get that same feeling in 2020 with no one in the stands because of COVID-19. The fans at Yankee Stadium created electricity that day in July. To have two perfect games in the span of a year and a couple of months? Are you kidding me? These guys were special, and I guess that's one thing they say about baseball: each day you never know what you're going to see. Somebody might hit four dingers, or someone might throw a perfect game. To top it off, Yogi and Larsen were there to witness it.

A couple of weeks after the perfect game, Coney had an awards ceremony in our clubhouse at Yankee Stadium. Two lunch tables were set up with approximately 40 gift boxes stacked on the table, and he was giving everyone these beautiful Ebel watches. On the back of the watch was engraved your name, the date, and "David Cone perfect game." During the ceremony, he said, "Jeff Mangold, I don't believe I'm giving you a damn watch." With some cuss words mixed in, he made guys laugh by razzing me a bit. That was how our relationship was, and he did give me one of those watches, which I still wear.

In his 2019 book with YES analyst Jack Curry, *Full Count: The Education of a Pitcher*, Cone wrote that I got to the Yankees and had not paid my dues, didn't ride the buses in the minor leagues, that I was over in New Jersey training some fat ladies, and then came over here to work for the Yankees. I guess he had no idea how many years I had spent working at Nebraska without getting paid and then the University of Florida and that I was with both the Yankees and the New York Mets for nine years in the major leagues before joining that Yankees squad. I'll leave it at that.

He was a prankster, that's for sure. Right from the get-go in 1998, he told me, "I'm gonna ride your ass." The other players liked that. Coney wouldn't berate me, but he would give me hell. He was a little bit of shit-stirrer like that.

In spring training of '99, it was the first week, and I was putting the pitchers through a very tough conditioning set. It was really hot. Their conditioning program for that day admittedly was very tough to complete. Players were required to run 100 yards, then turn and jog back to the starting point. This was repeated 10 times, and their running times were monitored. There was a lot of stopping and starting. Coney said, "Goddamn, Mangold, it's the fifth day of spring training. Are you trying to kill us?"

He said a lot of expletives. It was for the other guys to laugh about it. So that didn't bother me at all. I liked it and gave it right back to him. "Let's go Coney," I said. "Move it!"

Cone is so great behind the microphone on the YES Network, but I don't think a lot of people know how fun-loving he is. Another thing that stands about Cone's perfect game was that Javier Vazquez started for Montreal that day, and when you look at those two pitchers, I always thought stylistically that they had very similar deliveries and repertoires. Vazquez came to us a few years later in 2004. He had that little hitch and pause in his delivery that Coney had, too. He always looked just like Cone to me on the mound, though he got roughed up on that day for six runs in seven innings.

Coney's slider definitely was on that day. It was breaking a foot and a half, like a Frisbee. Those Expos hitters didn't have a chance. He didn't have a full count the whole day, and you could tell when he dropped to his knees and fell into Joe Girardi's arms how much the perfect game truly meant to him, especially at that stage of his career. Yogi and Larsen being there only made it more surreal. Wells even called him in the clubhouse afterward from a road trip with the Blue Jays. And while 1999 was a very different season from the one we enjoyed the previous year, Coney's gem would send us on our way to another perfect ending.

13

The Rocket and
the 1999 Season

I WAS INTERESTED TO SEE HOW THE TEAM WOULD REACT AND HOW I would react when we reconvened in Tampa, Florida, for spring training in 1999. It almost was like having that really good steak or having a bottle of a really great Cabernet. You know what winning tastes like now and you want more. You've seen what it takes to get there and what it takes to seal the deal, so hopefully everyone is on board and still pushing in the same direction. We learned right away, however, that it would be a very different year on many levels compared to the mostly smooth sailing that what we'd experienced in 1998.

There were so many land mines for the team to navigate in '99 both on a personal level and from a baseball standpoint, but it made repeating as champions that much sweeter and satisfying. We'd been in spring training only a few days when general manager Brian Cashman pulled off the blockbuster trade for Roger Clemens on February 18, and then barely one month later, the entire team was floored when Joe Torre revealed that he'd be taking a leave of absence to receive treatment for prostate cancer, leaving beloved bench coach Don Zimmer running the team for nearly two months.

Torre still definitely communicated quite a bit to give Zim some assistance, and Zim had managed before in a few stops and had some success. The players really adored him, too. It always helps to be liked. With some managers, people just don't give the extra effort for them, With Zim that wasn't a question. They played hard for him. Plus, we still had the rest of our veteran coaching staff led by Mel Stottlemyre and Willie Randolph. We still had Jose Cardenal, Tony Cloninger, and Chris Chambliss.

Torre often has said that he regrets handing the reins to Zim because it put Zim right in George Steinbrenner's crosshairs. They had a couple of public blowups early that season, and I'm sure it was stressful for Zim. He was not a young pup anymore and he certainly had a different personality than Torre, who'd let things roll off his back and not let them bother him as much. Zim was more confrontational, and it didn't take long for him and Steinbrenner to lock horns. A major blowup occurred one day after the infamous incident involving Hideki Irabu, the so-called "Nolan Ryan of Japan," whose rights Steinbrenner had acquired in 1997 from the San Diego Padres.

Irabu actually won 13 games during our record-setting 1998 season. He was never the fittest athlete, and the next spring there was the massive blowup, in which Steinbrenner infamously called him a "fat pus-y toad." (It rhymes with fussy; he didn't actually call him a pussy.)

It was the last game of spring training before we'd fly out that night for the West Coast, where we were going to play two exhibition games at Dodger Stadium before opening the season up the coast in Oakland against the A's. Irabu didn't cover first base during this exhibition game against the Cleveland Indians, and Mt. George absolutely erupted about him to the media. Our flight was held up for over an hour, as we all sat around the clubhouse in Tampa waiting for the situation to be resolved.

Everyone was excited that we finally were breaking camp, and we were all dressed sharp, wearing sport coats, because we'd be traveling. Irabu was in the manager's office with Steinbrenner and with Cashman for quite a while. Torre wasn't there because he was undergoing chemotherapy. We waited and waited and finally we left and headed to the airport for the long flight to L.A. while Irabu stayed behind in Tampa to work with organizational pitching guru Billy Connors. By the next day, Steinbrenner was telling reporters that he wanted Irabu back in the rotation as soon as he was straightened out and could join the rest of the team. Zim was fuming when reporters informed him of Steinbrenner's intentions. "I'm the manager," he said. "George has fired better people than me, and I'm not going to let him walk all over me!"

Right away, it became very territorial. I think the saving grace was still having Torre in his ear, and having guys like Randolph and Stottlemyre helped Zim hold down the fort until Torre came back on May 18 in Boston. During the time period when Torre was receiving his treatments, I would meet him at Yankee Stadium twice a week when we were home to work out with him.

Even after the Wells-Clemens trade, the returning guys were extremely focused, and that started from early on in spring training. I don't think anyone was necessarily burned out or fatigued from all the celebrations, late-night TV show appearances, or speaking engagements from the offseason. You could tell immediately these guys were still hungry. Bernie Williams was re-signed after almost bolting to the Boston Red Sox as a free agent. Scott Brosius and David Cone also were re-signed that winter. Along with Paul O'Neill, Tino Martinez, Mariano Rivera, and Derek Jeter, there was a group of leaders, and people just fed off them and followed their lead.

From my perspective, though, Irabu always was a challenge. He smoked a lot...like all the time. When we were playing Toronto in spring training at Dunedin, Florida, Irabu came out of the game after throwing his scheduled three or four innings. Several players who came out of games would come out to me for further conditioning, and I'd always be in one of the outfield corners, depending on which dugout we were using. They came to me for conditioning work and then would go back into the clubhouse to shower up and wait for the bus to take us back to Tampa. Irabu didn't understand English well at the time, but he had his interpreter, George Rose. Hideki would run so slowly, and I'd have to get on him, telling him, "What are you doing? This isn't doing you any good." But he just stuck with that approach. I did all I could to get him healthier, so he could be more productive. I really got on his ass because I knew there was a lot of pressure from the top for him to deliver after Steinbrenner gave him that big contract. When it came to the conditioning aspect of it, he was just a very low-effort, low-intensity guy. He was traded the next winter, and I was extremely saddened to hear that Irabu was found dead by what was ruled a suicide in Los Angeles in 2011. That's such a tragedy.

Irabu was only one of several major storylines unfolding during that '99 camp. Another was Darryl Strawberry trying to come back from colon cancer the previous fall and regain strength while he was still undergoing chemotherapy. It ended up being Straw's final year in baseball. He tried to make it back from his cancer treatment, but I don't think he ever really regained his strength after that winter of chemo. He started the year on the DL and then he got arrested for soliciting sex from a policewoman posing as a prostitute in Tampa in April. He only appeared in 24 games that year in September and got only 49 at-bats, but he was on the postseason roster and earned another World Series ring before retiring.

Earlier in the year, Straw and I got into a clubhouse spat. This was during his final spring training. He was out on Field Three. It was time for conditioning work, and Straw was on the field working with a personal trainer on the far side of the field. At that point there wasn't any mandate from MLB about having only team personnel on the field. It was getting to be a problem for me with a couple of players having their trainers there. Jorge Posada had a trainer there, and Jeter's guy was around sometimes, too, albeit never on the field. Jeter usually would go through drills with me.

The players' ability to utilize personal trainers onsite had been discussed before, and instead of me approaching Strawberry directly and trying to eliminate this problem, I thought this was a decision for somebody above me to lay down the law. I went to Cashman, who said he'd take care of it and talk to Straw about it. Well, the next day before practice, Coach Cardenal came up to me and said, "Hey, if you haven't seen Straw yet, he is looking for you."

His locker in spring training was a few down from mine. He was in that corner immediately when you entered the room and took a hard right. I was the second locker in. All of a sudden, Straw just laid into me. "I'm gonna deck you," he said. "You're going behind my back to Cashman and telling him about my trainer?"

I just tried to defuse the situation, but he was hot and bothered, for sure. It was in front of the majority of the team, too, right in the clubhouse. You're not going to get in a fight with Straw. That's not a guy you want to get in a brawl with, as the Baltimore Orioles found out the previous year. You have no choice but to deescalate the situation. I just kept saying, "Darryl, please relax."

He was hot, but he finally simmered down. He ended up apologizing to me a few days later and he actually did some very good work with me after that. It definitely was a new year because in '98, my first year back, everything was smooth and easy. Regardless, I felt like that was a big moment for me and how I handled it. I'm sure everyone wanted to know how I was going to handle being in a verbal spat with Strawberry. When he said he was sorry, he came into the weight room and said, "I apologize for getting steamed."

From then on, we were good to go. To that end I always believed it was important to draw the line regarding having friendships with the players. You couldn't get too close to them, go out to dinner, have some drinks, or really socialize with them. There had to be a line because the next day I'm the one who's telling them to be on time and telling them what we're going to do. I had friendships, and there was respect, but you let them do their own thing. You didn't necessarily want to hang out with them and vice versa.

Clay Bellinger—whose son Cody won National League MVP in 2019 for the Los Angeles Dodgers—made the team as a 30-year-old utility player after more than a decade in the minors. It was a great story. When we flew out to play the exhibition games against the Dodgers, we hadn't made the final cuts yet for the roster. Clay Bellinger was one of the last guys vying for a spot. Everybody liked Clay, who was a hard worker and a jack of all trades. I know the moment was coming that someone was going to get bad news. I was out in the dugout in the afternoon at Dodger Stadium, and nobody else was around. It was just the ground crew watering and dragging the field. I enjoyed those moments so much. All of a sudden, Clay Bellinger came out and leaned up against the wall by the bat rack and he started crying. I was thinking, *Oh Jesus, this guy just got bad news.*

It was the opposite. He was crying from being so happy after getting the news from Zim that he made the team. He came out to just savor the moment and have some private time. That was another one of those human moments in athletics that you don't forget. Some of the greatest things you witness are not even from the games. Years later to see his son, Cody, become the game's big star in that same stadium, that's a truly cool connection.

Wells was like a hero around town. He had pitched the perfect game the previous year, won a World Series, and was kind of a folk hero. Right at the beginning of spring training, Clemens came in to replace him in the rotation. By his lofty standards, Clemens had a bad year in '99, finishing 14–10 with a 4.60 ERA. He was trying to feel his way through a new team, new teammates, a new environment, and he also was fighting a hamstring issue most of that year.

We'll get to the PED stuff and the arrival of his personal trainer Brian McNamee a bit later, but initially as a strength coach, I was interested because there was all this talk about Clemens and his legendary workout regimen. I wanted to see it for myself. Before he even walked in the door, I had heard of his admiration for Nolan Ryan and how Ryan was considered somewhat of the pioneer for sports-specific strength and conditioning for pitchers. I told Clemens right from the beginning, "Whatever I can do for you related to how you like to work and your programming, I'll push you as hard as you want. I'm here for you. Just let me know. My time is your time, as with everybody else, but whatever I can do to assist you, I'll do it."

As it turned out, there never really was any consistency of work between us that year. He was doing a lot of his work somewhere else, and the next year, his personal trainer, McNamee, came in. Clemens was much more consistent from that point on. He apparently needed his buddy. It didn't seem like he was comfortable the whole first year. That is at least not until he won that clinching Game 4 of the World Series in our sweep of the Atlanta Braves that October. Before that he just wasn't a huge factor for us. He had his moments and he pitched okay at times, but he certainly wasn't the impact pitcher that everyone expected. His struggles somewhat continued the whole year, but he did try to be a great teammate and was full of stories and one-liners. He also exuded confidence, professionalism, and leadership. The numbers that first year just didn't add up to what he wanted, what he'd done in the past, or what the Yankees were expecting.

The first time I met Clemens was years earlier in his rookie year of 1984. The Red Sox came to Yankee Stadium, and Clemens and Dwight Evans were using our weight room. I remember Clemens was this big bright-eyed Texan, but he meant business even then. He was carrying with him what was called an EZ Curl bar with which you can perform various strength training exercises, especially targeting the upper body. You don't see many guys walking around or bringing their own bars to road games, that's for sure.

Before McNamee got there the next year, there weren't any specific issues between me and Clemens at all. There wasn't anything negative or derogatory between us. There was no animosity. He never said to me, "that's not the way I do it." Like I did with most guys, I just let them go and do their thing for whatever made them comfortable. I eyeballed things and made suggestions. I did approach him a few times that first year because I'd noticed a lack of consistency. I tried to invite myself into his domain and his trust. He was reluctant to let me in. He definitely had some sort of leg issues that year, too. I just don't think he was ever right that whole year.

He redeemed himself in the World Series, but probably the worst moment for him was when he started up in Boston in Game 3 of the American League Championship Series against Pedro Martinez. The Fenway fans were relentlessly chanting at him. It was his first playoff start against Boston as a Yankees pitcher. He gave up five runs in two innings, and it was like the biggest party in Beantown since our forefathers threw crates of tea into the harbor. His wife and kids were taking abuse from the fans, too, but they were just relentless on Clemens. Everybody was screaming "Rog-er, Rog-er, Rog-er" in a sing-song fashion, dragging out his name, even long after Torre removed him from the game. I don't know how anyone can block that out entirely and keep their focus, but you have to do it. The Red Sox took that game 13–1, even though we won the series in five games. The city of Boston wanted a pound of flesh, and that's what it got.

In the World Series that year against the Braves, however, Clemens started Game 4 and he pitched one-run ball into the eighth inning against John Smoltz. We'd won it all again after all we'd been through that year. People would say that's the moment he really became a Yankee. He finally earned his pinstripes after a rough, uncomfortable year for him. Sportswriters could see it. Torre and the coaches could see it. His teammates could see it. It was obvious. He was just trying to adapt. It's not easy for a big star when he gets thrown into the melting pot or the cauldron of New York.

It didn't hurt that there were so many stars on that team to divert some of the attention from him. For instance, 1999 was Jeter's best season statistically. He had career highs in batting average (.349), OPS (.989), home runs (24), RBIs (102), hits (219), and runs scored (134). Jeter also did one thing that I've never seen another right-handed hitter do at Yankee Stadium. He hit a home run to the upper deck in right field. I had never seen that done before there even with the short overhang, and I told him so afterward. I think he, too, knew how rare a feat that was. It was an up-and-away fastball—perfect for that inside out stroke of his, and he got all of it.

Jeter always had a special relationship with Zimmer, who became a story in the first game of the playoffs that year against the Texas Rangers, when he got drilled in the head by a foul ball off the bat of Chuck Knoblauch in the sixth inning of Game 1 of the American League Division Series. He came back the next night wearing an Army helmet with the NY insignia on it. That also ended up being the impetus for the Yankees to finally add dugout railings at Yankee Stadium. I was standing probably 10 to 12 feet from Zimmer when he got hit. Everybody ducked and got out of the way, but I don't think Zim even saw it coming. All of a sudden, he went right from the seated position in the dugout and fell forward. It was probably a three or four-foot drop to the padded base of the dugout. Everyone was concerned because of his history with head trauma from getting hit multiple times as a player in the 1950s. He was laying there on the rubberized floor, and trainer Gene Monahan and I walked him up the ramp back to the clubhouse. I came back out and was standing by the bat rack. Yogi Berra was standing right behind me and he said to tell the guys that Zim would be right out. Yogi was so relaxed and under control, and then a little while later, Zim came back to the game with a big ice pack.

The story of that season also was heartwarming because we had several players who lost their fathers during the year. Scott Brosius had to leave the team for a bit in September. Luis Sojo's dad died during the playoffs, and then there was Paul O'Neill. Paulie's dad died on the day of Game 4 of the World Series, but he played that night. He has said his father would have wanted him to play and he broke down, crying on the mound in Torre's embrace after the final out was recorded.

It felt like life's difficulties were rearing their ugly head all year, but we just had to be professional enough to keep going and realize that life was precious and that we're lucky to be in that position. That really united that team. Torre would say so often through the years, "You don't know how lucky you are to be at this point." He stressed that idea during each postseason and especially during each World Series appearance. "You guys don't know how hard it is to get to this point. Don't take it for granted," he said. "This doesn't come around all the time. Enjoy it and relish it. It's very special."

It was said in a congratulatory way, but it also forced us to realize how fortunate we were. He would never say anything negative while addressing the group. He didn't want to have any negative thought in anyone's mind. I tried to deal with players in a similar manner. If, for example, it was a hot, humid day, I would never say, "Oh, it's a hot one, fellas."

One day that season it was a blistering hot game, and for our stretching that day in warm-ups, I went to our equipment manager, Rob Cucuzza, and got out all the winter gear. I put a winter coat on as if it was a 32-degree game. I had a hat and gloves on, long coat, and sweatpants, as if the heat didn't matter. I think they appreciated that. Players need to be shocked every once in a while, and it was occasionally important for me to break the routine and add a little humor to help keep the guys loose.

When we first arrived at Turner Field in the buses for the World Series, we got out and walked toward the entrance of the locker room. There were parking spots under the stadium marked off for the Braves' administration, their GM, and other executives and so forth. There were labeled parking spots, and those labels were on the walls. One sign said, "Reserved for Hank Aaron. Don't even think about parking here." That's certainly understandable considering his stature in the game.

Before Game 2 at the World Series that year, they announced MLB's All-Century Team. Prior to the game on the infield, they had this giant platform and a ceremony introducing so many of baseball's all-time greats, including Stan Musial, Bob Gibson, Sandy Koufax, Pete Rose, Yogi, and other legends I watched growing up. I didn't introduce myself to anybody, but that was quite a moment. To see all those Hall of Famers together in one spot was wild. I also remember hearing later about TV announcer Jim Gray asking Rose about his gambling problems. After hitting a walk-off home run against

Atlanta's Mike Remlinger in Game 3 of that series, Chad Curtis told Gray he wasn't going to speak to him because of the way he spoke to Rose.

Before the Game 4 clincher against Atlanta in 1999, we didn't have the pitchers run before the game. Usually, we would run every day right before the last hitting group. For some reason I just had a feeling. Jeff Nelson asked me why we weren't going to run that day. I said, "No, we're good today." That was my way of saying I fully expected them to win the game that night. And we did.

Torre always addressed everybody very calmly, but I also remember him during that series essentially telling the team: "Fellas, I just want to tell you I've gotten numerous calls from managers and friends in the game who respect the way we play and the way you run everything out and hustle. You guys continue to play like that, and people in the game respect you for your all-out approach to go hard down the lines."

That kind of pumped the guys up a little bit. Players want to be respected. That group was one of the most professional groups I can remember on a regular basis. Our guys knew we were better than other teams. We wore teams down and did what we had to in order to win. Winning the first two games on the road against the Braves meant we could win it all at home. Those first three years after I returned, we won in three different cities. Winning at home in '99 really gave me the opportunity to share it with my family. In '98 we were in San Diego and in 2000 we beat the New York Mets at Shea Stadium, but the '99 clincher was at home. That was wonderful for my family. We took some amazing pictures with my mother-in-law, my wife, and my kids.

What a phenomenal feeling to be out along the right-field foul line with Yankee Stadium packed. The players were getting their running in, and I'd look up to the family section and see them up there right before the game started. That was special. I'd always tip my cap to let them know I saw them. Seeing them waving, smiling, and jumping around was fabulous, especially after hearing your name over the PA system announced by the legendary Bob Sheppard and trotting out to the first-base line with your teammates.

That championship was such a distinct experience from my first one. The 1998 season definitely was magical, and I'd never experienced that before. The second one maybe was more of a validation. It was also a little bit of a relief. People doubted if we could do it again, especially with everything we went through that year. They always say the second one is harder to win than the first one. And the third one would prove to be special for another reason.

Brian McNamee:
The Elephant
in the Room

THE DAY BEFORE SPRING TRAINING WAS TO BEGIN IN 2000, I WAS IN the weight room in Tampa, Florida. Brian Cashman came in and told me, "You're going to have an assistant this year."

This hadn't been previously discussed. There was no mention all winter of adding to the staff. During spring training camps, occasionally I would have an intern or two from the University of South Florida who would come in and help us, but once the season started, they wouldn't be around. I had always done the job alone. Thus, I was taken aback when I learned from Cashman that my new assistant for the 2000 season would be Brian McNamee.

I wasn't aware that he had been Roger Clemens' personal trainer from his days with the Toronto Blue Jays or even that they'd been working regularly with each other away from team facilities throughout Clemens' first season in New York. "Can you deal with this?" Cashman asked me. "Can you deal with having him as your assistant?"

Honestly, I felt like I had no choice. In my mind, we'd just won the World Series for the second year in a row and I thought, *Why rock the boat at all? We'd been doing pretty well.* Regardless, that was the start of McNamee being around for the next two seasons. We attended a meeting a couple of days later in the trainers' room with trainer Gene Monahan, his assistant Steve Donohue, and team physician Dr. Stuart Hershon just to make sure everybody was on the same page. Prior to walking into that meeting, Joe Torre came up to me and said pretty much the same thing Cash had mentioned, "Jeff, listen, if you don't think you can make this work, let me know."

I don't know if he wanted me to put the kibosh on it or not, but all I said was, "Joe, I'll make it work."

I would do whatever it takes. I'm not the decision-maker on that. I was on board, but the first inkling of the issues that were to follow—of a pro-McNamee sales job from Clemens within the team—came only a couple of days into spring training. We were out on Field Three, the pitchers had just finished with some conditioning work, and I overheard Clemens say to reliever Mike Stanton, "Mac has got a really great bike program. You should try it out."

That was the first indication to me that there could be some plan to undermine me a little bit or to push McNamee as an alternative for the players. Throughout that first year, I didn't really talk too much to McNamee. Once it was announced he was coming, I knew he definitely was going to be Clemens' guy. Still, there had been no point during the 1999 season—even with his struggles to adjust to pitching in New York—when Clemens said directly to me, "I need McNamee here."

From what I've read—I didn't see or know about this meeting firsthand—but it was following that playoff appearance against the Boston Red Sox, when the fans were chanting, "Rog-er, Rog-er," that he supposedly got together with Cashman and said, "I can't go through this anymore. I need to have my guy." Cashman essentially testified to this encounter more than a decade later during Clemens' 2012 perjury trial for allegedly lying to Congress about PED use in 2008. (Clemens was acquitted in the case.)

Personally, it was disappointing to learn that any player felt he needed to have a certain individual around to succeed. I was determined to do whatever I could to make it work, but it was a strange feeling to have someone around the players besides me who had complete domain over these guys and their workouts. It didn't take long to realize that my voice wasn't the lone voice influencing other players on the roster. Either it was Clemens' voice or McNamee's voice, but you could tell they were trying to build their own unit of guys there, to build a camaraderie, and to align with McNamee instead of with me. My hands were somewhat tied, but I said I was going to work with it and I continued to try to do that.

I knew it was a matter of time before this arrangement was going to implode, and there were going to be problems. At the time I thought it was a short-sighted decision to bring in McNamee to take care of a short-term immediate issue—Clemens—rather than taking care of the entire team. They were gambling that there'd be no disruption, and it was a bad bet.

I didn't ever hear him say this personally, but in David Cone's book, he wrote that at all the spring training games, I would be wherever Torre was. If he was going to Bradenton, Florida, for the Pittsburgh Pirates, I'd be there. That would leave McNamee behind with the guys who weren't traveling. McNamee was out with the players stretching one day, and Coney got into a confrontation with him. His presence already was starting to be a small disruption, and I had to see if I could smooth it out and make things work for everyone on a professional level.

In Torre's book, *The Yankee Years* with Tom Verducci, Cone also was quoted as saying that guys like Clemens, Andy Pettitte, and Stanton quickly were on "Mac's program." He went on to say that McNamee "had some GNC stuff he was putting in shakes, creatine, or androstenedione, or whatever he could get over the counter at the time."

The players knew something was going on in that respect. Beyond Clemens, a lot of guys who were working out with McNamee like Pettitte, Stanton, Chuck Knoblauch, and Jason Grimsley ended up being named by McNamee in the 2007 Mitchell Report on performance-enhancing drugs. McNamee specifically testified that he injected Clemens with steroids more than a dozen times, a charge Clemens vehemently denied.

I gave depositions four different times in various court cases in the ensuing years, including three times with the FBI, regarding defamation suits that McNamee and Clemens filed against each other, as well as the aforementioned perjury case, following Clemens' testimony before Congress. The first conversation was with Clemens' lawyers, Rusty Hardin and Associates, and specifically the firm's director of investigations Jim Yarbrough. They called me and wanted to know if I'd speak with them. I agreed since I had nothing to hide. We ended up meeting in Ridgewood, New Jersey, in an office setting. I did not have a lawyer present with me. It was just me. "Listen, I've never seen anything illegal being done," I said, "or anything dispersed or presented to anybody regarding pills or shots or needles."

I told them what I've always said: just the story of having McNamee thrust upon me at the beginning of that year. We discussed the 2001 episode in St. Petersburg, when a woman alleged that McNamee had drugged and raped her in a hotel swimming pool, an incident for which no police charges ever were filed. They were trying to uncover any type of dirt they could use against McNamee.

I later met three times with the FBI: once at Yankee Stadium and then twice more in downtown New York at the FBI offices in 2012. The meeting in New York City included myself and an FBI agent in the office, and then also another three or four agents or investigators on the case joined in on a video teleconference from

Washington, D.C. They were asking me questions regarding whether I saw any needle marks on anybody, if I saw anything done in the locker rooms, and whether I had any inclination of any type of drug use. I had not, and my sworn testimony reflected that. I was being up front that I'd never seen any of this activity they were describing. If something was going on, I think these players were smart enough to avoid doing anything in-house at Yankee Stadium or at least in my vicinity.

All I said was there definitely was a groundswell toward guys being around McNamee and training with him. And that was part of a two-fold deal of both Clemens speaking with the guys, pushing them in that direction, and then McNamee trying to convince them. He just wasn't a guy to be trusted, in my opinion.

McNamee also testified to federal investigators looking into Clemens' alleged drug use and to the Mitchell Report as saying that the drug use was widespread in the Yankees clubhouse before he even arrived. "Some guys were open about it, and some guys weren't. You wouldn't believe the shit they were taking," he said. "It was like horseshit. They didn't know the toxicity levels. They were taking Ritalin, oral steroids. They were taking stuff that was bad for them."

He made it sound like he got them on better programs once he arrived. Part of my response to that is you have to consider the source. I think he's been caught telling quite a few untruths. I think he was having conversations with the players, as if to say, perhaps he could provide them something that would help them.

My attitude was let's keep the ball rolling here, play the game. I'm not the judge and jury, and if there's nothing right in front of me, I'm not going to go searching. I'm not a cop. So there was a very fine line there. There was another quote from McNamee in Torre's book: "Mangold was Joe's guy. Roger would tell the players to go see me, not Mangold."

Did I start getting the sense that certain guys were starting to drift away from my message and seeking out McNamee? Absolutely. You had Stanton, Pettitte, Grimsley, and Knoblauch, and all these guys ended up stubbing their toes along the way and wound up being named in the Mitchell Report. David Justice was another one of 22 former Yankees named in the Mitchell Report. He came over to us in the middle of the 2000 season in a trade with the Cleveland Indians, and he and dozens of others were alleged to have bought PEDs from a former New York Mets clubhouse employee named Kirk Radomski, allegations that Justice has vehemently denied.

When I was with the Mets, Radomski essentially was the clubbie who'd make food runs for the players. He also worked in the laundry room, cleaning players' gear. Justice started working out hard after he arrived, saying he was trying to get some consistency, but it was mostly with McNamee, not with me. Grimsley also was close with McNamee and was listed in the Mitchell Report as a ringleader among the players in terms of PED use. I don't know if that was surprising or not, but he was very physical, very into martial arts, and known as being a tough guy.

There was one episode in Detroit in the weight room of the visitors' locker room. Grimsley and Mac were working out. McNamee was training him quite hard, and I had told both of them to start reducing the poundage of what they were doing because it was getting toward the end of the year. Grimsley was squatting on what's called a Smith machine and he had probably 350 pounds on there, which is a lot, and taking a lot of effort to do it. I blew up at these guys. It was blatant disregard for my authority. I didn't go to anyone about it, but I essentially said, "Listen, I told you guys: you shouldn't be doing this at this point of the season."

This was just defiance. It was someone who was working out with McNamee and not following along the lines of my recommendations. Still, there was never a time that I went to Torre, Cash, George Steinbrenner, or even to Monahan to try to blow the whistle of what was going on. I did not. I think it was evident in a lot of people's eyes, and no one really said anything about it. I did send an email about McNamee to Cashman in 2001, but that was not about any sort of PED involvement.

In the email I sent to Cashman, it solely was about my complaints about some chiropractic moves that he was performing on Clemens and other players. It was to the point that I was moved enough to contact Cashman, but it wasn't any implication of anybody involved with PEDs. It was more about insubordination. When I met with the FBI, they came up with that email, mentioning McNamee. I know Mel Stottlemyre also had voiced his displeasure about McNamee's involvement with some of our pitchers and him making suggestions about their mechanics.

On the flip side, nobody in the front office came to me either to say, "Jeff, there's rumblings around the league now of widespread steroids use, especially after the Mark McGwire and Sammy Sosa allegations started going down." Nobody asked me, "Do we have a steroids problem? Are guys doing PEDs?"

It felt strange. It was sort of this see-no-evil, hear-no-evil, speak-no-evil kind of thing. It was like, we're winning and making millions upon millions of dollars. Why light a firecracker under the whole thing? I would say we probably didn't want to know basically. It was somewhat of a blind eye turned to the whole thing. You also could see the trend of guys wanting to train with McNamee, and that ended up leading toward similar situations as we moved forward with the organization. The same thing happened in the ensuing years with Bobby Alejo, who was Jason Giambi's personal trainer, and then when Alex Rodriguez arrived in 2004.

Even Jose Canseco showed up in the Bronx late in that 2000 season as a waiver claim. Canseco and McNamee also were friends from previous years because Canseco had been with the Toronto Blue Jays at the same time as Clemens. They were good buddies. Canseco has been very open about talking to various players about steroids and PEDs, but I didn't get the sense he was necessarily pushing guys on the Yankees to try different drugs. He was only with us a few months, but he definitely was a free-wheeling guy.

I know that it's a very political explanation that I'm giving, but those are my statements and the same ones I made to the authorities. I didn't see anything. I didn't see anything being handed out, being taken orally, or being injected. What I saw was a groundswell toward movement to work out with McNamee, and he was the one who claimed he provided PEDs to Clemens and the others. In hindsight, do I firmly believe all of that was going on even if it was not happening in the clubhouse? It sure looks that way. I still can't say that with 100 percent certainty, though, because I honestly didn't see any of it. If I had seen something, I would have acted upon it, either telling them to knock it off and/or going to management because that would be a legitimate problem. It's a very touchy subject, but it was a very tough time for me to go to work and to know that the team was getting pulled sideways in that way.

Previously it was all my responsibility. But it was getting away from me. Did any of the main guys on those teams come to me and say: "We are in your corner," while these other guys were drifting toward McNamee? No, not really. But everybody saw what was happening and felt it. Because Clemens was such a powerful force and such an influential personality, people were not going to be quick to confront him or go up against him. It was very frustrating. I knew it was a matter of time before it would implode.

Torre had said to me at the very start if this arrangement wasn't working out to let him know. In fairness, there never was any point in which I said to him I was losing control or that it wasn't working. In spring training of 2001, however, after McNamee had been there a full year, Steinbrenner initiated one conversation with me in the trainer's room in Tampa. Similar to what Torre and Cashman had said the year before, Steinbrenner told me, "Jeff, if things don't work out here with [McNamee], let me know about it."

My only reply to him was, "George, a leopard doesn't change its spots."

He just looked at me, and I think it was understood that I was saying that things weren't going to change with McNamee. That was the first and only conversation I ever had with Steinbrenner about him. I never went back to him and said this isn't working out. I wanted to be professional about it and follow orders. I took Steinbrenner's comment as a challenge more than a question. It was kind of like, "Okay, make it work."

Even with Clemens enjoying his best season in pinstripes in 2001, going 20–3, and winning the AL Cy Young Award, McNamee was fired after the season ended. It certainly would not be the last time I had to deal with personal trainers or superstar players who would be linked to PED usage during my Yankees tenure.

The Subway Series

WHAT COULD WE POSSIBLY DO TO TOP WINNING THE WORLD SERIES in my first two seasons back with the New York Yankees? How about a three-peat—joining the 1972–74 Oakland A's as only the second team in baseball since the Yankees had won an unprecedented five straight championships from 1949–53—to do so? How about this one coming against the crosstown New York Mets in the first Subway Series since 1956—two years before the Brooklyn Dodgers bolted the outer boroughs of New York for Los Angeles?

Back in the summer, we had played a split doubleheader on Saturday, July 8 against the Mets. The twin bill featured a day game at Shea Stadium as part of a regularly scheduled three-game interleague series, but on Saturday night of that weekend, we also bused back to the Bronx to make up a game that had been rained out in June. The next morning we were back in Queens for the series finale, and I was putting in some work in the Shea Stadium weight room with a few of our players before the game.

Lefty relief pitcher Mike Stanton was part of our group, and I don't necessarily remember who else was there with me, but according to *The New York Times* account of the incident, Jason Grimsley and David Justice, whom we'd picked up from the Cleveland Indians earlier in the summer, were the others who were present. Steve Phillips, the general manager of the Mets, called me out into the hallway and very sternly told me that the Yankees were no longer permitted to utilize their weight room. It was standard practice by then to have an allotted time for the visiting team to use those facilities on the road, but this was the Mets being completely petty over what had happened the night before involving Roger Clemens beaning Mike Piazza.

The weight room at Shea was adjacent to the Mets' clubhouse and right next to the food room, and I had a working familiarity with the setup there from my prior employment with them.

We were in there for probably no more than five or 10 minutes when someone affiliated with the Mets came in and said to me, "Steve Phillips needs to speak with you out in the hallway right now."

I stopped what I was doing and walked out of the room, and Phillips immediately barked at me, "What the hell do you think you're doing?"

Phillips was the front-office person I'd met with when I was let go by the Mets four years earlier. So our relationship probably wasn't the greatest anyway. "You guys came over here to work out after what happened last night? Get the hell out of here," Phillips said. "Get these guys out of here."

Rather than get into an argument, we went back to our side, and our guys were laughing and shaking their heads. Joe Torre was walking by, overheard me telling one of the players about it, and immediately wanted to know what happened. I told him we just had been kicked out of the Mets' weight room and that Phillips said it was because of the Clemens-Piazza incident the previous night. Torre's comment later to the press was, "Well, we like to conduct ourselves with class." He just shook his head like there was nothing we could do about it. It was idiotic and too bad, but we didn't make a big deal out of it, even though our guys were incredulous. It was just another part of the fiasco that came to a head in October.

Brian Cashman's trade for Justice in June—sending Ricky Ledee and minor league pitchers Jake Westbrook and Zach Day to the Indians—really had provided a boost to our lineup earlier that summer. He was a winning player who'd appeared in the postseason every year from 1991 to 1999 with the Atlanta Braves and then Indians, and his lefty swing and professional hitting approach stabilized the middle of our lineup with guys like Paul O'Neill, Bernie Williams, and Scott Brosius spending time on the disabled list. Justice finished the regular season with 20 home runs and 60 RBIs in only 78 games with us after the trade and then he was named the MVP of the American League Championship Series against the Seattle Mariners after hitting a couple of huge home runs.

Our other big acquisition that summer, however, didn't fare as well. Left-handed starting pitcher Denny Neagle was just a strange, very quirky guy and he did not pitch well for us. What he was most noted for—and guys asked him about it as soon as he came over in a trade with the Cincinnati Reds in July—was that he could do this incredible impression of a train whistle. It sounded just like a freight train was coming. He also was a very superstitious guy. When he was pitching, he'd have his glove facing a certain direction on the bench each time and then before he'd go out to the mound he'd take a swig of water and shoot it out through his front teeth like a fire hose. He turned out to be another in a long line of guys whose career just didn't work out in New York. He just did not perform well. He was gone by the next year. After his ERA reached almost 6.00, he only lasted half a season. It was more entertainment than production, that's for sure.

During that season and the run-up to October, we took our foot off the gas in September and limped through the final month by losing 15 of our final 18 games to finish 87–75. It was the first time that the guys weren't closing the deal, finishing people off, and just coming up short.

Some were fluke losses, but I also felt like maybe you didn't see people getting as upset about each loss, which was different from previous years. It took on a life of its own until Torre finally called a meeting, saying basically: "Enough of this, you guys are sitting around waiting for the switch to click back on, but it doesn't work that way. Let's get it going. The playoffs are coming up in less than a week."

Well, we definitely did turn it on, eliminating the A's and Mariners in the playoffs. Then came the Mets.

Of course, for me, that matchup had some extra kick to it because I had worked for that franchise previously. Phillips was the GM there, and Bobby Valentine was the manager, and they had let me go. I really wanted to win this one. The buses would arrive at Shea, drop us off by right field, and we'd walk across the field to get to our dugout and into the visiting clubhouse. I remember saying hello to some of the ground crew, especially their longtime head groundskeeper Pete Flynn, whom I had been friendly with from my time there.

I was totally hellbent to beat these guys and the team that fired me. There was a little extra in it for me. Obviously, it was the World Series, and it was a Subway Series on top of that, but this was more than special to me. It was personal, too. I've heard both Torre and Jeter say this: there was more pressure in that World Series than any other we played. It was like we'd never hear the end of it in New York if we lost to the Mets. Without a doubt, that was true. You could just feel it. It didn't have to be spoken. If we lost, it would be a scar for life. No matter how many other World Series we won, people always would remember us losing to the Mets. George Steinbrenner definitely felt the way, too.

Game 1 was the one in which O'Neill had a heck of an at-bat, an 11-pitch walk in the ninth inning against our old nemesis, Armando Benitez, who by that time was the Mets' closer. That led to a game-tying sacrifice fly by Chuck Knoblauch and ultimately a game-winning RBI single by Jose Vizcaino in the bottom of the 12th inning.

The second game featured the Clemens-Piazza histrionics involving the broken bat, and Clemens impressively went on to pitch eight shutout innings before a late Mets rally against our normally sturdy bullpen fell short. We still won 6–5 and grabbed a 2–0 series lead.

The Mets took their first game at Shea 4–2, but then Jeter rifled a leadoff home run in Game 4 against Bobby Jones to get us back on track. You could tell that no matter what: Jeter intended to swing at the first pitch. I'm sure he was looking for a fastball, and he got it. He was determined to put us on the board right away. It was one of so many remarkable things that only Jeter would do.

A few of the game-winning hits in that series came from unheralded players like Vizcaino and then Luis Sojo in the Game 5 clincher. The fact that these unsung guys, the bench players, were doing it showed that no matter how many big names are on a team you need everyone on the roster to contribute. That's the kind of deep team we had. With that 16-hopper up the middle that got through, Sojo showed what a pro he was. He could do a lot of little things. He wasn't usually the story, but boy, he could play winning baseball. He was a good leader who'd also get in people's faces when he needed to but also a funny guy.

What was great about Sojo from my professional perspective was that he was known for being a little heavy sometimes—he had a big rear end on him—but he got serious at the end of that season and really committed to working out. He began the year with the Pittsburgh Pirates, was let go before the start of that season, and then found his way back to us in August. He really started taking care of himself in preparation for a moment like that. It all really tied together when he got the chance.

The other story for the Subway Series was the flood situation in our clubhouse at Shea during the sixth inning of Game 4. Not surprisingly, Steinbrenner had a take-charge reaction to it. I was in the trainers' room, talking with trainer Steve Donohue while he was working on someone. I was sitting on one of the tables in there, and then all of a sudden, a deluge of water came crashing down from the ceiling. It was one of those corrugated drop ceilings, and that also crashed down on us in soggy chunks. A pipe had burst, and we were completely shocked, but we started to grab whatever trainers' equipment we could because everything was getting drenched.

I wasn't even aware at the time that Steinbrenner was watching the game in the main part of the clubhouse. The room we were in was offset from there. Steinbrenner immediately started organizing everyone and taking action, barking orders at all the clubhouse workers who were in there. I don't think there were many—if any—players in there at the time because the game was going on. Steinbrenner ordered us to get all the equipment up off the floor and pick up everyone's shoes because the room was going to flood quickly. He was giving directions, and I was among those going around grabbing shoes and their other belongings that were on the floor.

Eventually, the ground crew came in with a bunch of sandbags and bags of that drying agent that they use during rain delays, and we tried to stack them to make a levee from the trainers' room so the water mostly would be contained in there, keeping it from totally destroying the locker room, too. Minutes later the fire department showed up, and I would say the water had to be gushing for at least 10 minutes before they got there. It wasn't sewage and fortunately didn't stink to holy hell, but this water kept coming and coming. Finally, somebody found the control valve. By that time, the locker room already was soaked.

We were getting all of our sofas moved out into the hallway. Steinbrenner had ordered them brought over from Yankee Stadium earlier in the series because he'd wanted all of our players to be as comfortable as possible. All of a sudden, there had to be eight to 10 firemen in there, and huge hoses were brought in to suck up the water. The firemen were in full fire gear with helmets on. Everybody was busy trying to clean everything up. They took care of everything pretty quickly, and by the time the game ended, you couldn't really tell what had happened except for the floor being wet.

Meanwhile, the final innings of the game were being played out, and we pulled out a 3–2 victory after Mariano Rivera recorded the final six outs to move us within one win of another title. Players did interviews out on the field because the media wasn't allowed in the wet clubhouse. My lasting memory of that night still was of Steinbrenner, who walked around afterward handing out $100 bills to the clubhouse people and even to the firemen, tipping them, saying "Make sure that everyone gets one of these." That's Steinbrenner for you. He was so difficult to deal with but could also be very generous.

One night later we won Game 5 at Shea when Williams flagged down Piazza's line drive for the final out to clinch our third straight World Series championship. It was so satisfying for me—both personally and professionally. Little did I know at the time, but this would be my final championship—even if the following year might have been our most memorable trip to the World Series of them all.

16

9/11

WE WERE SUPPOSED TO HAVE A HOME GAME AGAINST THE CHICAGO White Sox the night terrorists attacked our country on September 11, 2001. I was doing my normal morning routine before going to the ballpark. I went to downtown Oakland, New Jersey, to grab a cup of coffee and a newspaper. I went into this little deli, and people in line to pay for their food and coffee were fixated on the television behind the counter. As I was pulling into the parking lot, I had heard on New York radio station WCBS that there was a report of a small plane that crashed into the top of the World Trade Center. When I walked into the deli, somebody said, "That was no small plane that hit the tower. That was a big jet."

That's when all hell started breaking loose. I gathered my purchases and got back in the car to drive home. We were having a lot of construction being done at our house at that time, and on my way home, the radio station confirmed that it was an airliner. There were two ladies I knew on my street who were getting in their morning walk. They didn't have a radio with them, and this was before everyone had cell phones. So I told them, "You probably haven't heard, but you might want to get home right now. The World Trade Center was hit by a jet plane."

I arrived home, turned the TV on, and decided we had to pull the kids out of school immediately. Sean, my oldest of three children, was in the local middle school, and as I arrived, other parents already were arriving. Everybody was beyond flustered. I went into the office to sign him out, and initially when Sean heard his name called to come to the office, he thought he was in trouble. As soon as I saw him, I think he saw the worry on my face. "Sean, we're going home," I said. "This is going to be a day you will never forget in your life. We're okay. We'll go get Jaime and Jesse out of the grade school and go home."

In the next several weeks, Joe Torre and several players made their way down to Ground Zero to visit firehouses. They met with first responders and the families of those who lost loved ones in the attacks. I kick myself now for not trying to find a way to be a part of that. At the time I was just trying to be with my family as much as possible. The New York Yankees reconvened for a road trip that began on September 18 in Chicago, followed by three games in Baltimore. Our first game back at Yankee Stadium was on September 25 against the Tampa Bay Devil Rays. This was four days after Mike Piazza's home run had lifted the Mets and the city in the first sporting event back in New York after the attacks.

Of course, there was some trepidation about flying and there was so much uncertainty. What if the enemy targeted a stadium during a game being played by the Yankees? Driving across the George Washington Bridge to and from New Jersey was surreal. There were soldiers and military trucks on each side of the bridge, especially on the Jersey side. I won't ever forget my first time coming into the stadium, coming across the bridge. I forced myself to look down to the Hudson River, and you could still see smoke smoldering. It was an eerie feeling of sorrow and disbelief.

Unlike many in the area, I'm fortunate that I didn't have any family members or friends who perished that day, but there were a couple of people from the church we attended, the Church of the Most Blessed Sacrament, who passed away in the towers. As far as first responders, firemen, police, emergency detail, I didn't really know anybody.

The rest of that fall, I'd get chills when chants of "USA, USA" would take over the various stadiums at home or on the road. Every day there were always touching tributes and moments of silence. Because of that, the playoffs that year took on a totally different feel. We had won three straight World Series, but when you talk to anyone who was part of our team that year, they'll say how there was such a pall cast over everything. We really tried to rally around the sadness and win it for the city and for the country to provide whatever small lift we could for people who were hurting. Everyone just understood that. That was the maturity of our team. Even though there were a few different personalities, it was still a veteran-led club, and so many things didn't have to be spoken.

We dropped our first two home games to the Oakland A's in the American League Division Series. As we boarded our buses after Game 2 outside Yankee Stadium's executive offices, getting ready to fly to Oakland, we were extremely quiet. Adjacent to our bus a few feet away, Oakland's team was giddy and upbeat. You could see them moving around with the lights on in their bus, slapping each other on the back, laughing, just having a good time. That was a young, fun team, and they were always kind of free spirits. You couldn't blame them, and I understood that, but I was just pissed, and the rest of our guys were too.

Three or four feet from these guys laughing, we were boarding our bus without saying a word. We knew what we were up against. Nobody said anything. You couldn't miss the juxtaposition. Oakland wasn't trying to rub anything in our face. They were just being themselves. It wasn't deflating, but we realized we had been pushed to the brink in a way we hadn't been the previous three years. Once we got out to Oakland, Torre made a subtle comment that I'll never forget. He posed a simple but savvy question in the clubhouse. "Hey, Bernie, Paulie, do you guys want to hit when we get back to the stadium before Game 5?"

That was if to confidently say: we'll win the two games here and finish them off at home. That showed his extreme confidence in the team. It was like there was no doubt in his mind that we'd win the two games. It was a great use of sports psychology. He said it so calmly, which is his way. It reminded me of the Muhammad Ali quote that I had painted on the wall in the Yankee Stadium weight room: "The fight is won or lost far away from witnesses, behind the lines, in the gym and out there on the road, long before I dance under the lights."

Game 3 was the most intense game I'd ever been through. Torre used to say you would sell your soul for a run or a hit in a certain instance, and this was that type of game. We ended up winning 1–0 on only two hits. Jorge Posada hit a fifth-inning home run, and Mike Mussina pitched a gem.

Most memorably, Derek Jeter made his famous flip play, in which he ran to the first-base line to scoop up an errant relay throw by Shane Spencer and flipped the ball to Posada to nail Jeremy Giambi at the plate. Mussina pitched seven scoreless innings, and Mariano Rivera worked the final two to close it down. The flip play occurred in the seventh inning to preserve the one-run lead, and it was the essence of Jeter always being in the right place at the right time.

Giambi rounded third, and Spencer overthrew both Alfonso Soriano and Tino Martinez, but Jeter came cruising across the infield as if he had a purpose for what he was doing. Giambi didn't slide, and it was a bang-bang play as Posada swiped him with the glove. We couldn't really see if he was safe or out, but when home-plate umpire Kerwin Danley signaled the out, we knew Jeter had saved the day. Derek was just being Derek. He had such a feel for the game. Even after a play like that, he'd just shrug his shoulders as if to say, "I was where I was supposed to be. This is what I'm supposed to do."

Throughout the postseason, there were bomb-sniffing dogs coming into the clubhouses, combing through our bags and lockers. There was security everywhere, and it was pretty intense. We won the next game 9–2 and then headed back to New York—just as Torre had suggested—to close them out.

Next, we were on to Seattle to face Lou Piniella, rookie sensation Ichiro Suzuki, and the Mariners, who had won 116 games to break our '98 American League record of 114. We didn't really use that as a big rallying cry. It was more unsaid because there never was any negativism, especially from Torre.

I know guys specifically mentioned that Arthur Rhodes had been shooting his mouth off about us, and they wanted to get the lefty reliever into the game and take him deep. We ended up doing just that when Bernie Williams clubbed a game-tying home run against him in the eighth inning of Game 4, and then Soriano belted a walk-off homer against closer Kaz Sasaki in the ninth. We sealed our fourth straight trip to the World Series the next night. We had so much momentum, especially at home, especially that year. There was such an unmistakable surge of energy from the crowd and the city behind us after 9/11.

Our World Series opponent had a personal touch for me. The Yankees were facing the Arizona Diamondbacks, and between my jobs with the Mets and the Yankees, I had interviewed with them to be their strength and conditioning coach. Former Yankees manager

Buck Showalter had been hired in 1996 to be their first manager, and 1998 was going to be their first year playing games as an expansion team. I flew out to Phoenix to interview with Showalter and general manager Joe Garagiola Jr.

I got there the day before the interview. I like to go outside to run and I did so from my hotel down near the stadium site, which was being built at the time but wasn't yet completed.

I ended up running through a construction gate area and ran around part of the inside of the stadium as it was being built. I stopped and tried to figure out where home plate would be. One of the first things I jokingly mentioned when I interviewed with Showalter and Garagiola was that they might want to update their security because the previous I day I was out running and got into the site. They ended up going a different direction, hiring somebody else, but to come back to that stadium a few years later for the World Series was pretty cool.

Arizona's co-aces, Curt Schilling and Randy Johnson, were superb against us in the first two games there, downing us 9–1 and 4–0 to give them a quick, 2–0 series lead. After we lost the first two games in Arizona, we headed back to New York. President Bush was there to throw out the first pitch before Game 3. On the off day between games in the buildup to this historic moment, I was standing down the right-field line, and all of a sudden, a maintenance crew golf cart came up behind me. The man driving stopped very close to me; he was a member of the Secret Service. He said to me he'd be in that cart the next night when the president walked out to the mound to throw out the first pitch. In the back of it, where the ground crew usually kept shovels, would be a folding accordion-style piece that was made of lead and covered with AstroTurf. If something went down with the president, this agent would be the first person out there and would put this cover over him for protection.

In the walkways and down by the weight room and the tunnel where the batting cage was in Yankee Stadium, there were Secret Service people everywhere. There were even Secret Service in the weight room and every 10 yards or so down the hallway. I didn't see President Bush before the first pitch, but we've all seen the videos and heard the stories about Jeter hanging out with the president in the batting cage area. Jeter kiddingly advised him to throw from the top of the mound and not to bounce the pitch or risk the fans booing him. The president admitted that was a lot of pressure coming from Jeter, but he knew he had to throw from the top of the mound.

When President Bush emerged from the dugout, I was standing probably 35 yards away on the right-field grass and down the first-base line. We all stopped what we were doing. I was just in awe of the moment. Looking around Yankee Stadium, you knew there were snipers everywhere, and helicopters had cordoned it off as a no-fly zone. It wasn't a simple moment in sports. It was a moment of world and national significance. There are so many instances of me being incredibly lucky to be in these situations. I was an eyewitness to a lot of amazing sports history, but this was different. I got to see a lot of famous people throw out the first pitch, but it was nothing like this. There also was the famous bald eagle named Challenger that would fly in from center field for this game and various other games throughout the years. I remember them practicing that in an empty stadium, and this trainer would blow his whistle, and you couldn't really even hear it, but this gentleman would extend his right arm as a landing spot for the bald eagle, which is a symbol of America.

There were epic moments during the game, too. In Game 4 and Game 5, the two ninth-inning home runs by Martinez and Scott Brosius to tie those games and then win them in extra innings had Yankee Stadium shaking and absolutely rocking. I was there for some big Yankee moments, but I never experienced anything quite like that before or since, especially under the circumstances. Those two nights were absolute bedlam. When you factored in everything that the city and the country had been through, you had to pinch yourself. It goes back to the ghosts of Yankee Stadium or the ghosts of past players. Strange things happen in that stadium.

Both comebacks came against the same reliever, Byung-Hyun Kim, only adding to the craziness. During his Game 5 meltdown, Kim got down in a crouch on the mound and just held his head. He was in the middle of it and seemed to be succumbing to the aura and ghosts of Yankee Stadium. I remember the Diamondbacks came in for an interleague series the following year, and Kim recorded a save. He took the ball and chucked it over the wall in left-center field right onto the netting of Monument Park. It was kind of like he was trying to get payback against those ghosts.

Especially after everything that had happened with 9/11 and all of the heartbreak and sadness, even Hollywood couldn't script a believable story that the team from New York would experience those two nights. For it to happen the second night was insanity. Brosius wasn't the type of guy to showboat, but he knew it instantly. All of us knew it, too. The ball just jumped off his bat, and everybody jumped off the bench. Because Paul O'Neill was retiring after that season, the fans had been chanting his name from the stands for a couple of innings, even though we were losing. Win or lose, that was going to be his final game at Yankee Stadium.

Even down to his last home game, O'Neill was such a pro that he was going to do everything he'd done in the past. He came out for warm-ups, did his stretches, his runs, and his high-knee action. All of a sudden, he said to me, "Oh man, I forgot my belt."

I told him not to worry about it. I altered one of the clubhouse attendants, who served as a ballboy down the line. I told him to run into the clubhouse and grab O'Neill's belt out of his locker.

O'Neill's mind was elsewhere. He understandably didn't even get fully dressed that night. The love affair between O'Neill and those fans was special even if he tried to somewhat downplay it as much as possible. He was a prideful man, intense, and the fans legitimately respected and adored him. He came to play every day. He'd be out in right field, playing defense, and taking phantom practice swings. And I think he's taken that popularity to another level now by becoming a beloved team broadcaster.

To lose that World Series during such an emotional time with everything that was happening in New York and not seal the deal was devastating. Who would think that Rivera—of all people— would be on the mound when it happened in Game 7? After winning the previous three World Series, it's hard to put losing in that fashion into words. Game 7 was just a different feeling. Everybody was so emotionally spent. We got hammered 15–2 in Game 6, but we still had a chance at the four-peat.

To change things up, we had a short meeting before the game, and Torre called on trainer Gene Monahan to address the team. I think it caught Monahan off-guard, but being around for so many years, so many victories alongside legends from Thurman Munson and Ron Guidry to Graig Nettles and Goose Gossage, Monahan was the perfect person to offer a few words. He basically said this was a great spot to be in: one more game to become champions. In his heart, he said the players were already champions. It was short and sweet. That was a very special for Monahan. And to have it be a member of the training staff was special for me. Rivera spoke, too, and said it was "in God's hands."

Soriano went deep in the eighth inning to put us ahead 2–1, and it was just so intense. We were on the doorstep with the greatest closer of all time on the mound. The crowd was going wild even before Rivera gave up a leadoff single to Mark Grace.

He then made a throwing error to second base on a bunt play. Tony Womack, who came over to the Yankees a few years later, ripped a double down the right-field line to tie it, and I immediately had a feeling that things were getting away from us. I had a bad feeling. But if anybody was going to find a way to get us out of this, it was Mo. We brought the infield in, but then Luis Gonzalez, Martinez's childhood buddy from Tampa, Florida, hit a little blooper over Jeter's glove, and that was it.

When the game was over, I'm not the type of person to sit there on the bench and watch another team celebrate. As soon as that happened, I got up and walked into the clubhouse. Guys were slowly coming into the room, and Chuck Knoblauch was right next to me. Martinez was a couple of lockers away. These guys came in and just sat in their chairs facing their lockers, staring in silence for what seemed like forever with their heads down.

That whole run took so much out of everybody. There was such pain. That was the end of that era, in my opinion, the end of that run. Deep down I think people kind of knew that.

O'Neill and Brosius were retiring. David Cone was already gone. Obviously, the Core Four guys were still there, and we made the World Series again in 2003, but that was kind of the breaking up of the older portion of that group. Just the sorrow and the pain of not delivering New York a championship that year was hard for everyone to fathom. It was such a deflating feeling.

There were a few times during the end of that regular season when the clock eerily showed 9:11 while Kate Smith's recording of "God Bless America" played during the seventh-inning stretch.

Everyone on the team always wanted to win so badly, but that year extended far beyond winning it for ourselves. I've seen members of that team over the years say that losing that World Series has stuck with them as much as the years they'd won it all. Even though we lost, it was the run they remember most of all because of the impact it had on the city.

17

Boone Goes the Dynamite

WE FAILED TO REACH THE WORLD SERIES FOR THE FIRST TIME IN FIVE years in 2002. Even though we won 103 games in the regular season, it felt very much like a transition year, especially when we were sent home abruptly and emphatically by the Anaheim Angels in the American League Division Series. The stinging loss made the ride back to the World Series the following year that much more enjoyable, and players from the new guard like Mike Mussina, Hideki Matsui, and Aaron Boone resulted in some of the biggest moments of the year.

Before the 2001 campaign, we had signed Mussina, the Baltimore Orioles' longtime ace, to replace the departed David Cone. The next year we added slugging first baseman Jason Giambi to play first base after moving on from Tino Martinez. Still, we just couldn't recreate the same intensity we had previously once Paul O'Neill, Scott Brosius, Coney, Martinez, and even Chuck Knoblauch left. The makeup of the team changed, and it was hard to replicate what we'd lost.

Giambi came in and had a hell of a first year, blasting 41 home runs. Robin Ventura also came over from the New York Mets to replace Brosius and he hit 27 bombs with 93 RBIs. The lineup, even though Jorge Posada, Derek Jeter, and Bernie Williams were still there, sort of shifted to revolving around Alfonso Soriano and Giambi, a discernible change from what it had been the previous few years. More than anything, we didn't pitch well that October of 2002 against the Angels. Even gamers like Andy Pettitte and a returning David Wells got knocked around. They beat us three out of four and scored 31 runs in the four games, not exactly the playoff pitching we'd grown accustomed to during the championship years. Joe Torre said in a brief meeting afterward, "When it ends, fellas, it happens fast."

Not everyone, however, was ready for it to end. The 2003 season marked a return of the magic from the previous years. Japanese import Matsui announced his arrival with the great fanfare of a home run in his first game in the Bronx, and our midseason acquisition, Boone, knocked out the hated Boston Red Sox with an 11th-inning home run in Game 7 of the American League Championship Series to send us back to the World Series.

From Day One in spring training, I could just see Matsui's attentiveness and his ability to learn quickly. As an example, I'd put our players through some agility drills for them to work on their change of direction, and there would be some movements with cones set up and a pattern to the course. There has to be some ability to grasp the explanations both visually and verbally as I explained to them why we were doing certain things, how it was done, and what we were looking to improve. You only had to show Matsui something one time, and he would grasp it. His intellectual capability, his focus, and his concentration were extremely high even without really speaking the English language. Day in and day out, his preparation to play was exceptional.

He would arrive in the afternoon prior to batting practice and go through a series of stretching drills and a lot of movements to strengthen his core, abdominal, lower back, and ribcage areas. I learned some things from him, too. He showed me movements he'd done in Japan with great success. There were exercises that he would do daily that I really liked and began utilizing with other players and those I train even to this day. There even was one movement that works the oblique so well that I now call it "the Matsui." The exercise entails lying flat on your back with your knees bent, feet flat on floor, and arms crossing your body to hug your chest as if shivering from the cold. You begin by keeping your lower body— from the hips down to the feet—still, as you rotate your upper body to a position of 10:00. From this point you elevate your upper torso approximately 4" off the ground by utilizing your abdominal muscles. Upon reaching this point and keeping your lower body still, you swivel the upper torso from 10:00 to a position at 2:00. Then you lower your upper torso to the ground and repeat the movement going from 2:00 to 10:00. The prime movers are your obliques, which are vital in baseball performance of swinging and throwing.

After he arrived I even learned to count to 10 in Japanese from his interpreter, Roger Kahlon, so that I could count off Matsui's exercises and lifts when we worked together. He was so durable, too. He arrived, having played more than 1,200 consecutive games in Japan. Then he didn't miss a game in his first three years with us until he broke his wrist diving for a ball in 2006. In his first three years with us from 2003 to 2005, he appeared in 163, 162, and 162 games, which rarely happens anymore for any player. Matsui had thick, muscular legs and glutes, but he also was trim and lean muscularly. There was nothing he'd do physically that was wasted movement. He had a high pain threshold, too. The durable Matsui was a cerebral, smart player. He and I got along very well both personally and professionally. He was a complete professional in every way imaginable. He not only played every day, but also played hard every day. That's why his teammates respected him so much.

Speaking of durability, our four starting pitchers in 2003— Moose, Wells, Pettitte, and Roger Clemens—all threw more than

200 innings. They all made 30 starts and they each won at least 15 games. The fifth starter was supposed to be Jeff Weaver, who we'd acquired from the Detroit Tigers the previous summer. He was another bad fit for New York and got yanked from the rotation halfway through 2003, leading to the arrival of our next big Cuban signing, Jose Contreras. That was a much-ballyhooed pickup because we essentially stole him from under the noses of the Red Sox. They thought they had him signed as a free agent, but we landed him for $32 million over four years. That's where the Yankees got the nickname "The Evil Empire," which was a reference to the *Star Wars* movie franchise. One of the Red Sox owners, Larry Lucchino, dubbed us that because of the Contreras signing.

Orlando "El Duque" Hernandez ended up getting traded, so the two Cuban hurlers didn't get to work together in the same rotation that first year. One thing that amazed me about Contreras was that part of his warm-up routine was to grab his arms and have us pull them behind him—almost like when someone is arrested and being handcuffed. He'd then lift them up to where his arms were nearly at shoulder length behind him, which is tough to do. We would cross his arms, cross his hands, which means the range of motion in his scapular area—the upper part of his back and the shoulders—had to be phenomenal. He would love to have that done to him and always wanted to be assisted doing that. It was a comfort zone in his stretching routine. At first, it somewhat scared me. I didn't want him to get hurt doing that because it was almost taking him out of the normal range of motion for most pitchers. But it was something he'd done all the time in Cuba. He was a big guy—6'4" and 250 pounds—kind of cumbersome, heavy-footed, and not a real great natural athlete. Not that you have to be to be a good pitcher. I think it was a tough acclimation for him just with the massive headlines and the pressure. It was a lot to live up to. He actually had more success later in his career after we traded him to the Chicago White Sox midway through the next season.

Weaver also had his struggles in New York. He was really talented with great stuff, and when the Yankees traded for him in 2002, we thought he was going to be our next ace. Just like so many others, it didn't work. He was always like throwing gas on the fire.

In midseason 2003, we also traded a young pitcher named Brandon Claussen to the Cincinnati Reds for Boone, who didn't do much the last two months of the regular season, but he ended up getting the biggest hit of the year for us. Just as he is as the current Yankees' manager, he was an upbeat, cerebral, sharp guy, always aware of situations even if he was not performing well or doing much. His personality, awareness, and willingness to do little things to help a team succeed made him such a valuable addition.

Whenever we'd play Boston, the intensity of the games was so draining. The games were so long. These guys were professionals all the way, but you just get up for some teams more than others. We got up for the Red Sox even more than our crosstown rival Mets. That also was David Ortiz's first year with Boston after six mostly nondescript years with the Minnesota Twins. I have to give him credit because he became such a great hitter and such a thorn in our side the next few years. We easily dispatched Ortiz's former team, the Twins, in the first round of the playoffs, and it was on to Fenway Park with several subplots, including Clemens facing the Red Sox again after he'd been rattled off the mound in a start against Pedro Martinez in his first year with us in the 1999 ALCS.

The two All-Star pitchers were pitted against each other again in Game 3 at Fenway four years later, and the story became the bench-clearing incident involving Martinez and our 72-year-old bench coach, Don Zimmer. A former Red Sox manager, Zim was always getting on Martinez, always yelling at him. Martinez and

Posada also definitely had it in for each other, and that Saturday afternoon at Fenway, I was seated on the bench not too far from Zim. Martinez had buzzed Yankees outfielder Karim Garcia; the umpires eventually ruled that the pitch nicked his batting helmet. Clemens, Wells, and Posada were barking at Martinez from the dugout, and at one point Martinez pointed at his head, as if to say "Use your head," he said afterward. I think our guys took it more as a threat that he was going to hit Posada or one of our guys in the head.

The next inning Clemens threw a fastball that wasn't really even close to Manny Ramirez. It was more high than tight. Ramirez took two steps toward the mound, and that was enough for the benches to clear. Zimmer made a beeline toward Martinez just past the first-base line. In my role as strength coach, I can't leave the dugout. From my view, it was hard to see everything during the fight as it happened. I vividly could see Zim running out that way and kind of away from the cluster. He clearly wanted a piece of Martinez. It seemed like a path opened up for him and kind of like a matador, Martinez just stepped to one side and threw Zim down to the ground. Then all hell broke loose. When the altercation on the field stopped, our trainers Gene Monahan and Steve Donohue were with Zim in the dugout, tending to a cut on his face, and they walked him up to the clubhouse. They ended up taking him to the hospital on a stretcher, but he turned out to be okay, and we won the game 4–3.

Having started Game 3, Martinez and Clemens were back on the mound to lock horns in Game 7 in the Bronx. It's hard to imagine a more marquee matchup for a decisive game. First and foremost, we were down big against Martinez—5–0—when Giambi gave us some life with two solo homers in the fifth and seventh innings. It made the game a little more manageable and it set us up to come all the way back. Boston manager Grady Little definitely left in a tiring Martinez a couple of batters too long in the eighth. Posada dunked in a double to tie the score, and that hit was another of those moments in the Bronx that reverberated around Yankee Stadium.

Of course, everyone's primary memory was Boone's home run. Jeter has said that he told Boone: "Be ready, be yourself." Once again the ghosts came out to play. Tim Wakefield was pitching, so everyone knew what was coming on the first pitch. Just look for the knuckleball. Boone has said he thought about taking a pitch there as he was walking up to the plate, but he thought better of it. He thought, *No way, if it's there and I can square one up, I'm swinging.*

Boone actually had been slumping during those playoffs and was benched for that game. Enrique Wilson started at third, and Boone came in as a pinch-runner a few innings earlier. But that home run was just one of those high and majestic no-doubters. As soon as he hit it, the dugout erupted in complete euphoria. It wasn't a matter of whether it was far enough. It was just: don't hook! Pandemonium ensued. I drove home that night and went across the Macombs Dam Bridge to get to the Harlem River Drive on my way back to New Jersey. Driving home I was thinking to myself, *I can't believe that just happened.* Yes, we were going to the World Series again, but just how this game ended was one of those absolute head-shakers.

Then, of course, came the letdown. It was a quick turnaround to play the Florida Marlins, and I think everybody without a doubt was tired. If I was fatigued and mentally drained from the ALCS, I only can imagine what the players were feeling. In the dugout prior to Game 1 of the World Series about a half-hour before the game, you could just feel there was no electricity. We were in trouble. Even the home crowd seemed spent. How do you match what the team had just accomplished? That World Series almost felt anticlimactic after beating the Red Sox in the manner that we did.

We were up against this young Marlins team with the grandfatherly Jack McKeon as manager, and they had all of these hard-throwing young arms: Josh Beckett, Dontrelle Willis, Carl Pavano, Brad Penny, and Rob Nen in the bullpen. They also had a young Miguel Cabrera and Mike Lowell, one of our former prospects, anchoring their lineup. Lowell had been one of the first minor leaguers I met when I'd rejoined the Yankees in 1998. He was traded the next year for a left-handed pitching prospect who never panned out named Ed Yarnall. A few years earlier also had been dealt by the Mets in the Mike Piazza deal. When I got down to Tampa, I had a conversation with this young kid, and Lowell was telling me, "Jeff, I'm gonna make it. I'm so excited to be here at this level and I'm gonna make it. Whatever it takes, I'm gonna do it. I'm gonna be a player."

Such confidence and maturity in a young man are qualities that definitely stand out. He went on to great things with both the Marlins and later with the Red Sox. Having worked with so many athletes, I had a feeling that this prospect was going to be somebody. It's just too bad it wasn't with the Yankees. Lowell was a leader, too. He made four All-Star teams and was on the '03 Marlins team that beat us and then the Red Sox squad that won the World Series in 2007.

The Marlins definitely were a hungry team, but no one thought they'd even get to that point. It was like the Mets' team in 2015 that got to the World Series behind all of those young arms. These guys all were dealing against us in 2003. They also had Hall of Fame catcher Pudge Rodriguez behind the plate, leading that young staff. They wanted it more than us. They took us out in six games after Beckett shut us down on five hits in the Game 6 clincher on short rest. We just couldn't get anything done. Posada made the final out, a slow grounder to Beckett, and I didn't even wait to watch him be tagged out. As soon as Posada topped that ground ball, I knew it was over. I couldn't watch these guys celebrate, especially on our field.

That ended up being the last World Series the Yankees would appear in until 2009—three years after my second departure.

The Marlins have been a thorn in my side throughout my career. I just don't have good memories about their stadium down there. I was there when I got the phone call two years earlier that my father had died. Even though we didn't lose the series in Miami, facing them in what turned out to be my final World Series appearance as a member of the staff always stuck with me.

The Arrival of A-Rod

AS YOGI BERRA WOULD SAY, IT WAS LIKE DÉJÀ VU ALL OVER AGAIN. Just as spring training was about to start in 2004, the front office pulled off a blockbuster trade for one of the biggest names in baseball—and one who years later would be a poster boy for performance-enhancing drug usage in the game. It was just like the Roger Clemens acquisition in 1999.

Aaron Boone, the hero of the 2003 American League Championship Series, had wrecked his knee in a pickup basketball game in January, and suddenly we needed a third baseman. Alex Rodriguez and his agent Scott Boras were trying to force his way out of Texas just three years into the landmark 10-year deal worth $252 million he'd signed with the Rangers in 2001. A-Rod actually was set to go to the Boston Red Sox, but that deal was killed when the Major League Baseball Players' Association wouldn't allow him to rework his massive contract. George Steinbrenner and Brian Cashman swooped in and convinced Rodriguez to move to third base—because Derek Jeter was entrenched as our shortstop—and he agreed to make that position switch in order to get out of Texas.

We had to sacrifice Alfonso Soriano to get the deal done, and he had been one of my favorite players to work with during his first three years with us. He was so lean, so strong, so fast. Soriano had been a 30/30 player in each of the previous two seasons, meaning he registered at least 30 home runs and 30 stolen bases each year.

In 2002, his second full season in the big leagues, Soriano missed a rare 40/40 season by one home run (39 dingers along with 41 steals). While with the Washington Nationals four years later, he became only the fourth player in baseball history to join that exclusive club with a career-high 46 homers and 41 stolen bases.

Of course, A-Rod already had been another member of that power/speed fraternity, having notched a 42/46 season with the Seattle Mariners to join Jose Canseco (1988) and Barry Bonds (1996) as the only players to reach those lofty numbers in one season.

There was a ton of media coverage when Rodriguez showed up in Tampa, Florida. It even exceeded Clemens coming in or anybody else you could think of. This was the best player in the game, and at that time, there were no public reports of any of the PED issues that he'd have to answer to later in his career.

As far as A-Rod's relationship with me, it always was quite smooth. He was a very inquisitive guy. He'd ask a lot of questions. Even when he was with the Mariners, he always had great respect for Paul O'Neill and he would ask me specific questions about O'Neill's workouts. Rodriguez would watch how O'Neil would warm up prior to games, and that made a lasting impression toward his game preparation.

The first year there, A-Rod seemed to do most of his work with a personal trainer away from the ballpark. By that point you had to be official team personnel to be inside any of our facilities. In February of 2009, when he first got outed for his past steroids use by *Sports Illustrated*, a Dominican Republic-based personal trainer named Angel Presinal acknowledged that he'd worked with Rodriguez during his three years with the Rangers from 2001 to 2003. The *New York Daily News* also reported that Presinal, who had been cited in the Mitchell Report, which had come out in December of 2007, had accompanied A-Rod on the road for all of that season. That was the year after I'd left the team, but it would make sense that their working relationship away from our facilities would have been maintained during his first four seasons with the New York Yankees.

I already had been through a few seasons of dealing with personal trainers being forced onto our training staff, including Brian McNamee for Clemens and Bobby Alejo for Jason Giambi. To appease Giambi, following his signing as a free agent to a seven-year deal worth $120 million in 2002, the Yankees hired Alejo as an unpaid batting practice pitcher (meaning he was compensated by Giambi) so he could be a part of our regular traveling party. McNamee was gone after the 2001 season, and Alejo was brought in the next year. The difference between their presences was that McNamee's influence was spreading throughout the team while Alejo was essentially centered just on Giambi.

Even though it might have ruffled some feathers on my end, the bigger problem to me was that the players were seeing the Yankees caving in to cater to another newcomer. I don't think there were any public grumblings, but I knew some holdover guys were unhappy with the arrangement that some guys were getting preferential treatment. Either way, the change was just thrust upon me again. Alejo and Giambi were working together, but then the following year, Steinbrenner abruptly mandated before the start of spring training that Alejo would no longer have access to the field or the weight room and no longer would be traveling with us. It must have gotten back to him that other players were unhappy about it.

Along those lines, just like with Clemens, I approached Giambi when he arrived. I told him I was there to do anything I could to assist or help at any time of day or night. Things just never clicked between us, even though he had a tough time functioning without Alejo. Unlike McNamee, at least Alejo was not taking on other

Yankees for workouts. With McNamee it almost had been like a pied piper or a politician trying to garner support and votes. Clemens was promoting him and basically recruiting guys. Giambi was not doing that, nor Alejo was crossing any lines to do that. He basically was only there for Giambi, and that seemed to be understood from the beginning. After McNamee was gone, my interaction with Clemens didn't really change. His work, wherever it would be completed, would often be offsite with McNamee and not at Yankee Stadium. Even on the road, McNamee often traveled, and they'd work out at the hotels or at a private facility.

Once Steinbrenner took Alejo off the road and removed him from our team facilities, he was not as visible around the team. By then Giambi also was embroiled in the Bay Area Laboratory Co-Operative (BALCO) trials, which centered mostly around Bonds, the San Francisco Giants slugger who'd established the new single-season home run record with 73 in 2001. Giambi admitted to a federal grand jury in 2003 that he took steroids and human growth hormone while with the Oakland A's, according to transcripts of the testimony published by the *San Francisco Chronicle* in 2004.

None of that ever came up between us, but just from his physicality, you had to question some things. You'd see his baseball cards when he was a kid, and he certainly didn't look like the same person physically. There was no interoffice discussion or questioning. No one alerted me or asked me for my thoughts on the activity of what was going on with Giambi. It's a touchy subject, but there had to be some suspicion, of course. I never saw any of this activity personally.

From early on after Rodriguez arrived in 2004, I think he still was seeing his personal trainer away from our facilities. I never met him, but I do know that Jerry Laveroni, a member of the Yankees' security detail who traveled with us, snuck Rodriguez's trainer in to meet him at least once in a private room to stretch and assist him. That's the only time that I really saw him. This definitely wasn't Yuri Sucart, the cousin who Rodriguez talked about years later when he admitted his prior PED usage. It was instead a personal trainer who supervised and assisted his private workouts.

A-Rod was a position player who came prepared for a game like no one else, regarding getting warmed up, getting loose, getting a sweat going, and studying the opposing pitcher. He was more than just a student of the game and he was always prepared to play. He'd come into the weight room 40-to-45 minutes before every game to warm up. This pregame routine was by far the most extensive I had seen for a positional player. I don't think that part of it was PED-related. That was just him. Say what you will about him and some of things he's done, but he had an unmistakable consistency in his work ethic.

Regarding PEDs, like I said before with other people, I never saw anything hinting he was doing anything. There obviously was all of the speculation and reporting about him doing things that came out afterward. His being outed by *Sports Illustrated* and admitting his usage when he was with the Rangers happened in 2009, three years after I had left the Yankees. His PED suspension for the entire 2014 season for his involvement with Biogenesis, the anti-aging clinic in Florida, was long after my time there had ended.

More than anything, Rodriguez was trying so hard. Just like so many other guys, he was trying to find his way after coming over to the Yankees. It's always tough unless you have the personality that water runs off your back, and that was not A-Rod. I think he always was very aware of what people said about him, very astute. He was very aware of the fans, his contemporaries, and baseball history. You had to give him credit that he always was trying to get better.

By the time he got to us, he had some years on him and he was a little thicker than earlier in his career as a shortstop. He definitely wasn't stealing as many bases as he had during his 40/40 days. He always was concerned about his speed and he'd always ask me about his time getting down the line to first base. He'd run in the low 4s, like 4.15 seconds, which was still pretty fast for most guys from the right side. We'd always talk about running mechanics. He told me to let him know if I saw that he was doing or not doing something correctly regarding his form. He liked to talk about his speed and he was so light on his feet during his younger days with the Mariners. I saw him in the weight room in Seattle earlier in his career. He was the young stud everyone was talking about. Man, he got to the majors almost right out of high school and had a great frame.

Whenever we'd have a big free-agent addition or trade acquisition—whether it was Chuck Knoblauch, Hideki Matsui, Giambi, or Rodriguez—on the fifth or sixth day of spring training practice, we'd go over to the main field, and instead of me conditioning the guys, Joe Torre would run this one drill of having guys run the bases. Torre would have a talk at home plate, discussing the importance of base running, running hard down the line, and hitting the bag correctly with the correct foot and with a good angle. We went through some drills, and Torre would always convince the marquee newcomer—and this year it was obviously A-Rod—to lead off and show us how it's done. The guys who'd been there knew what was going to transpire. "Go ahead, Alex," Torre said.

Rodriguez chugged down to first base and rounded the bag and headed for second. I don't remember if he did a pop-up slide, but he ended up at second base. As soon as he rounded first, same as with Giambi or whoever else did it in previous years, Torre would tell everybody, "Okay, take it into the clubhouse. We're done." Here's our new superstar showing a lot of enthusiasm and intensity. Then when he got to second base and looked back, everybody was headed off the field. It was little prank to fool him, a welcome-to-the-team sort of icebreaker. It always worked because Torre sold it really well.

Rodriguez came in that year and hit 36 home runs, knocked in 106 runs, and scored 112 runs, but somehow that was considered somewhat of an off year by his lofty standards. It also was Gary Sheffield's first year with the Yankees, and he also had monster numbers in 2004, recording 36 homers and 121 RBIs while hitting .290, to finish second in the American League MVP voting behind Vladimir Guerrero.

Sheffield didn't work out much at all at Yankee Stadium, but he was one of those guys you definitely wanted to watch whenever he came to the plate. It was like with Jeter or Don Mattingly. Those guys would play every game the same—whether it was a big crowd, small crowd, a World Series in October, or a road game in Kansas City in June. When Sheffield was in the on-deck circle, he didn't really take a lot of practice swings. He would just stand there with his bat in his right hand in a relaxed pose, staring at the pitcher.

Third-base coach Luis Sojo would watch Sheffield just rip these wicked foul balls. Sojo would stand way out of the coaching box as a result. You had to make sure your eyes always were on Sheffield. This was before exit velocity became all the rage, but I would love to know Shef's career exit velocity. He just hammered the ball and ripped absolute rockets. There were no check swings or many cheap ones coming off his bat.

Ruben Sierra was on that team, too. In the latter years of his career, he really pushed himself to get in better shape, really working harder than he had in earlier years from what I understand. He slugged a huge three-run home run in the eighth inning against the Minnesota Twins to tie Game 4 of the 2004 American League Division Series to help us advance to face the Boston Red Sox again.

After coming over in 2003 as a free agent, John Flaherty also was with us that year as our backup catcher. He and I would stand together often by the railing by the bat rack. He looked strange out there in his catching gear. He wasn't a big guy, and the straps went around the back like an old umpire. But he had a few big hits, especially the night that Jeter flew into the stands against the Red Sox to catch a foul pop-up. Flaherty had the game-winning hit in extra innings that night. He was a true pro. A sharp guy and great teammate, he knew the game, and that comes through when you hear him now as an announcer on the team's YES Network broadcasts.

Aside from Mariano Rivera, our bullpen was overhauled that year. Tom "Flash" Gordon and Paul Quantrill were the primary set-up relievers that year. And Torre worked them hard. Quantrill pitched just about every other day, and it felt like the two of them were running out of gas by the time the playoffs came around. The bullpen had been such a strength for so many years, but other than Rivera, all of those relievers from the championship years were gone.

That also was the year that Andy Pettitte left to sign as a free agent with the Houston Astros. David Wells was gone, too, and so was Clemens. Orlando "El Duque" Hernandez was injured, so Mike Mussina was the only holdover in the rotation, and we otherwise had a whole new set of starters: Javier Vasquez, Kevin Brown, Jon Lieber, guys who were accomplished elsewhere. Vasquez started out well. He made the All-Star team, but then he endured a terrible second half. Lieber was coming back from a year off due to Tommy John surgery and he pitched okay. Brown had some decent moments, but in early September, he punched a wall while angry over a poor performance and broke a bone in his non-pitching hand. We also added Esteban Loaiza during the season. Although the staff wasn't close to the same level we'd pitched in previous years, we still won

101 games. We were up 3–0 in the ALCS against the Red Sox and one win from returning to the World Series.

By now we all know the details of how it fell apart from there. Even the ghosts of Yankee Stadium couldn't save us that year. Pinch-runner Dave Roberts stole second base in the ninth inning, and Bill Mueller tied Game 4 with a single against Rivera. Papi Ortiz homered in the 12th inning and then delivered the game-winning single in the 14th inning the next night. Curt Schilling shoved us in the bloody sock game in Game 6 to even the series, and then Brown and Vasquez got hammered in Game 7. The Red Sox went on to sweep the St. Louis Cardinals for their long-awaited first World Series title since 1918. So much for the Curse of the Bambino.

During one of the nights during the ALCS, we were on the bus leaving the right-field area at Fenway Park. I was on the family bus with my wife, and the Red Sox fans were everywhere, yelling "Yankees suck," giving us the finger. It's one of the few ballparks where there is no private entrance. The intensity of the rivalry is just unmatched. There's respect but also pure hatred.

Another anecdote that shows the intensity of the rivalry between the Yankees and the Red Sox involves reliever Tanyon Sturtze. The 6'5" pitcher was with us between 2004 and 2006, and we were at Yankee Stadium when Manny Ramirez came up to the plate. Before Ramirez would get into the box, he often stared into our dugout on the first-base side to the point where some of our guys would yell at him to get in the box. It was Manny being Manny, as they say, and he just smiled and nodded his head. It got to a point where Torre even mentioned it to everybody before the game, telling us to let Ramirez do his thing and not rattle his cage or poke the bear, if you will.

During that game Sturtze was on the mound. I was standing by the bat rack 10 feet from Torre. All of a sudden, Torre uncharacteristically yelled, "Manny, this one is coming right at you. Get ready!"

I couldn't believe it. Sturtze threw the next pitch, and it wasn't even close to hitting Ramirez. It almost bounced actually, and Ramirez just crushed it to the opposite field. This ball was inches off the ground—like off his shoe tops. From the dugout it looked like a golf ball coming off a tee. Ramirez was unbelievable. Torre just sat there shaking his head. He was the one who had been saying don't rile this guy up, don't poke the bear. We were all laughing at that.

To get access to the weight room in Fenway Park was always tough. You had to go through their locker room. It was tight quarters and wasn't real conducive to our guys being able to work out. I made arrangements with a place that's no longer in existence—the Gold's Gym on Landsdowne Street right behind the Green Monster. I would take guys like Matsui, Andy Phillips, and a few others there when we were in Boston. Jeter even came with us a few times.

One of the Red Sox clubhouse employees would take us through the bowels of Fenway out to the street level and across the street to this gym. There'd always be fans out there at the bars as we made our way across the street to this gym.

It wasn't ever more than three or four players, but there'd be a few of us working out in this public gym before the game. No one ever gave us any trouble. I think they actually were glad we were there. The guys often signed baseballs for the employees there. We would go train, and I'd tell the clubhouse kid to be back at the door by 4:30, they'd open it, and we'd come back in. There never were any incidents with fans crossing the streets. Maybe somebody might yell "Hey, Matsui!" or "Hey, Derek!" It was like seeing a Broadway star going in the back entrance. In a three-year span, we probably did that 20 times.

Based on the way we went up 3–0 in that ALCS, winning Game 3 at Fenway by scoring 19 runs, it certainly looked like we'd be going back for another crack at a World Series ring. No team in MLB history ever had come back from an 0–3 hole to win any postseason series. I don't think many people outside that Red Sox locker room believed it was possible. By the end of Game 7, a lot of our fans had left, and the Red Sox fans that were there took over the lower section of Yankee Stadium. It was such a strange feeling. It was the only time I can recall ever seeing that at a home game in all my years with the Yankees. Their fans were so boisterous.

It was disheartening and painful, but as everybody says, you try to not get too high emotionally when you win or too low when you lose. You just have to deal with it either way. The series just started slipping away from us, and once those guys got a little momentum, it felt like they finally had broken through the dominance of Rivera. We were all shocked and frustrated that we didn't seal the deal, especially against them. The previous year we were the ones who were joyous after the Boone home run. Tim Wakefield had to walk off the field with his head down. The next year, we just had to take it. That was the closest to securing a fourth World Series ring that I would get with the Yankees.

Celebrity Encounters

BY THE NATURE OF MY POSITION, I INTERACTED WITH AND BUILT personnel relationships with some of the biggest names and stars in baseball throughout my time with the New York Yankees. That's from Yogi Berra, Billy Martin, Dave Winfield, and Don Mattingly to Joe Torre, Derek Jeter, Mariano Rivera, and Alex Rodriguez. The list certainly did not end there. Winning the championships we did, I got to participate in multiple visits to the White House, with both president Bill Clinton and George W. Bush. The latter even brought us all into the Oval Office, which was a very unique and awe-inspiring experience.

I also had the opportunity to meet some huge names from the field of entertainment.

In 1986 I had the chance to represent the Yankees at a Special Olympics event at the United Nations in Manhattan. Also taking part were Manute Bol, the 7'7" rookie NBA star from the Sudan, and prominent actors Christopher Reeve, who played Superman on the big screen, and Arnold Schwarzenegger, the former Mr. Universe and the future governor of California whose breakout movie *The Terminator* had hit theaters two years earlier.

I didn't meet Reeve that day. That meeting would come several years later, but he was there for the festivities. This was almost a decade before he was paralyzed in a horse-riding accident. This probably meant more to me, but the strength and conditioning coach for the University of Maryland football team, Frank Costello, also was there. Mostly, we were all waiting for Schwarzenegger to show up. When he finally arrived, we were told that he was going to address the crowd, and Costello, Bol, and I were going to do some exercises to show these young athletes the correct form and technique for lifting and training.

Shortly before we started, I excused myself to use the restroom and walked down the hallway to find one. I went to push the door open, and it wouldn't open. I pushed it again, and all of a sudden, a guy with a thick accent said, "You have to pull it."

It was Schwarzenegger, so here I was feeling like a little weakling in front of Mr. Universe or an idiot for not realizing how to open the door. After opening the door, Schwarzenegger held it for me, and I went in to use the restroom. He went in there just to change his shirt and put on a Special Olympics T-shirt. He was just a mammoth man with a huge chest, arms, etc. I joked with him, "Arnold, is that shirt even going to fit you?"

"They always fit. I always squeeze them on somehow," he replied.

It was a rather embarrassing moment. That was the only time I ever met Schwarzenegger. I was the only person there from the Yankees that day. It was quite a function and quite a memory. Though I didn't get to meet Reeve that day, I was fortunate to get another opportunity to speak with him at Yankee Stadium in the early 2000s. I just had finished stretching the team for a Saturday afternoon game. This familiar-looking young lady was standing on the field with credentials, and I was curious who she was.

I went over and introduced myself, and it ended up being Reeve's wife, Dana. This was a few years after he'd suffered his serious injuries. I had just read Reeve's book called *Still Me*. I was captivated speaking to her and how courageous the two of them were. I told her that. "Boy, I'd sure love the opportunity to meet your husband if he's around," I said.

She turned and pointed up to one of the luxury boxes above home plate at Yankee Stadium. "Well, Chris is up there right now and he's watching batting practice," she said. "If you have some time, let's go up and talk to him."

When I'd finished my pregame work, I went upstairs, and it was just myself and Reeve sitting there together in one of the boxes. He obviously was in his wheelchair with his breathing apparatus. We just talked briefly, and he wanted to know who some of the harder working Yankees were on the team. I mentioned Jorge Posada, Andy Pettitte and Jeter just to throw out a few names. He basically told me, "You guys have quite a team, you guys are really winners, and you really get at it. You make the Yankees fans proud."

I told him how proud I was of him and his courage and his fortitude to overcome his accident and still be a tremendous leader, a tremendous spokesperson, and an example for paraplegic people. He did such a great job raising all that money. That was quite a day. And it's so cool that I got to meet both The Terminator and Superman.

Reeve died in 2004 at age 52, but the final movie that he directed was an animated film set at Yankee Stadium named *Everyone's Hero*. It featured the voices of Rob Reiner, Whoopi Goldberg, Robin Williams, Mandy Patinkin, and even a brief cameo from Torre.

Another cool meeting was with actress and activist Jane Fonda during my first go-around with the Yankees in the 1980s. She and her husband Tom Hayden were on a tour to visit every major league stadium in the country. He actually was dressed to shag fly balls out in the outfield. I was stretching the team and getting ready for batting practice and again saw a young lady standing over by the dugout. I knew right away it was Fonda. She stands out. We ended up sitting down and spoke for a while in the dugout and then we went into the weight room. She wanted to see our setup. This was when she was first getting into going into her exercise kick and her aerobic workout videos. She was enthralled with strength training of athletes. We never connected to do any business together, but it sure was fun to meet her and to show her some of the workouts we did.

We were in Detroit to play the Tigers on Opening Day on April 6, 1987. Their organization had invited our entire team to Joe Louis Arena to watch the Marvin Hagler–"Sugar" Ray Leonard fight on closed circuit TV. We had an afternoon game and then we went over to have dinner and watch the fight. About half our team was there. We were in the locker room of the Detroit Red Wings, and they had a big screen for the viewing there in the arena. There was an array of food and drinks for us. Tigers manager Sparky Anderson was there, and so was Kirk Gibson.

Huey Lewis and the News were going to be playing at the area the next night, and Lewis also happened to be there. They had a couple of huge albums out and were, of course, famous for the hit song "Power of Love" from the popular film *Back to the Future*. I sat by Lewis for a while watching the fight, and we chatted. He's a great guy from the San Francisco area and a huge baseball fan. It was quite a nice gesture for an organization to do for us. It was great. The welterweight and middleweight classes in those years featured Hagler, Tommy "Hit Man" Hearns, Leonard, Roberto Duran, and Wilfred Benitez, and those fights among all of those men were unbelievable. By the way, I think Hagler got screwed that night, losing a split decision to Leonard.

Not all of my brushes with celebrities were from the entertainment field. One of the coolest things when I first got to the Yankees in 1984 was that the former Heisman Trophy winner from

Ohio State in 1955, Howard "Hopalong" Cassady, was one of our spring training instructors. George Steinbrenner obviously was from Ohio and he had been a former college football coach, but fans might not know that Steinbrenner and Hop were great friends for years. He never bragged about his past accomplishments and he was just a rugged son of a gun. You looked at him and realized the pounding that he must have delivered and also received during his playing days. His body was ravaged. He was a good guy, and the players and coaches all respected him. Hop also was a coach at Triple A Columbus for a while, so he was in spring training with us every year. Before I got there if there was any attempt at conditioning or formal exercise in previous spring trainings, he would try to assist guys and make sure they warmed up correctly. He never was anything but gracious with me, and I always appreciated that.

Trainer Geno Monahan was a huge fan of NASCAR and IndyCar racing and very often because of him we'd have various drivers who'd won the Indy 500 or the Daytona 500 at Yankee Stadium after they'd won those races. Monahan was nothing but professional his whole career and so respected by everyone. He always helped me along, giving me pointers, telling me what to do. At the same time, he got out of the way and let me run things. I would mention to him any new nuances or programs that I would want to integrate regarding team warm-ups and conditioning, and he was all for it. He gave me carte blanche and was very trusting and professional with his approach. As somebody working directly with the medical staff, it was so important to have a line of communication, and that was always there. Monahan was so into racing that he even served as an athletic trainer for the NASCAR team of Hendrick Motorsports and was part of the team's pit crew.

The first time I laid eyes on Jose Canseco and Mark McGwire was when we were out in Oakland in August of 1984. They would win back to back Rookie of the Year awards in 1986 and 1987, but McGwire was their first-round pick that year out of USC, and I guess the A's brought them in for a press conference or to take batting practice. The Yankees were by the batting cage, preparing for our batting practice, and the A's were hitting first. Even though people had started hearing about Canseco and McGwire, none of us had ever seen them. These guys were hitting rockets for home runs. Most power hitters would hit majestic fly balls, long home runs that hit the stands and bounced. The budding sluggers were ripping line drives that were hitting the walls and the seats and making such noise with what they call now exit velocity. Our guys all just stopped and watched. I was trying to stretch guys out, and nobody was paying attention to me. They were just fixated on Canseco and McGwire. I'd never seen anything like it.

Being in big games, especially the World Series, also would draw a lot of celebrities. I was in the locker room in San Diego in 1998 before either Game 3 or Game 4, and all of a sudden, Kirk Douglas was just standing there. He died in 2020 at 103, so he would've been 82 at the time. He was with an entourage, though I don't believe his son, Michael Douglas, was with him. He had just a very familiar face that you can't mistake. He was part of Old Hollywood, when movie stars were movie stars. Even though he was that kind of legend, even he wanted the feeling of what it was like to be in the Yankees' clubhouse. It was kind of strange to think that people for decades would pay to see him, but he was coming to see us. You're not going to say no to Kirk Douglas.

Remember when Jeter crashed into the stands to catch that foul pop-up against the Boston Red Sox in 2004? Well, the next day at Shea Stadium, everyone was wondering if Jeter would miss a few games. When it came time for us to stretch as a team, we were behind the batting cage, and the players were stretching with bands on the ground. I had to have security mark off a location for us because there were so many photographers/media. As I was on the ground barking orders, Jeter was right next to me, and I looked over, and famed director Spike Lee was laying on his stomach taking pictures no more than two feet away from us. Lee kept saying, "Derek, you're the man."

Billy Crystal was another movie star who was around a lot. He was friendly with Torre. He walked into the clubhouse after David Wells' perfect game in 1998 and went right up to Boomer and joked, "I got here late. What happened?"

After we defeated the Seattle Mariners in the 2001 American League Championship Series, we had a workout day at Yankee Stadium before Game 1 of the World Series in Arizona. Crystal was dressed in a Yankees uniform that day. We were down the line in right field, and the team circled around me for our stretching routine. On this beautiful, sunny day, I was in the middle and had sunglasses on, and out came Crystal. "Hurry up, get over here. I'm your worst nightmare," I yelled to him at the top of my lungs.

That was the line from the character Curly played by Jack Palance in Crystal's movie, *City Slickers*. All of a sudden, Crystal went from this little jog to an accelerated run. That moment of me calling him out was fun, and some of the guys got a kick out of that. Later on during batting practice, we'd talked quite a bit, and he was saying how he played celebrity softball, and one of his hamstrings had been bothering him. We started talking about different exercises he could do for his legs.

Obviously, with as many big games as we appeared in, we had the opportunities to see some musical legends perform the national anthem. One that really stands out was Ray Charles singing

"America the Beautiful" before Game 2 of the 2001 World Series in Arizona. They had a platform set up by home plate. I was again down the right-field line getting the guys stretched. It ended up being just Bernie Williams and I out there by the time Charles started playing. Williams, who went on to an accomplished second career as a jazz guitarist, was in awe of Charles being there. A stealth bomber came zooming overhead the ballpark just as Charles was finishing singing. You heard this loud hum, and it was like a ball of fire going across the sky. It was a very powerful moment.

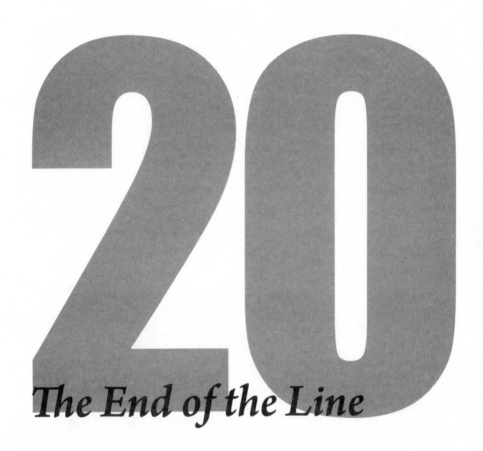

20

The End of the Line

THE STING OF THE COLLAPSE FROM A 3–0 LEAD IN THE 2004 AMERICAN League Championship Series against the Boston Red Sox carried over into the next couple of years, even though we won at least 95 games and finished in first place in the American League East each of those two seasons.

Bernie Williams dropped off from his years of excellence until the New York Yankees signed former Red Sox nemesis Johnny Damon for 2006 to replace him in center field. The organization didn't even offer No. 51 a guaranteed contract for 2007. Tino Martinez also came back for one final go-around in 2005 after playing two seasons with the St. Louis Cardinals and another with his hometown Tampa Bay Devil Rays. Martinez also just wasn't the same player anymore. Those two players had been so locked in and productive during the dynasty years, but there's always a natural drop-off from that norm. It's usually a quick fall. Martinez had been a great player, but he wasn't necessarily a natural athlete regarding speed, agility, and explosive jumping ability. I think players who do have that athleticism have a bit of a slower decline. More natural athletes like Dave Winfield, Rickey Henderson, and Alfonso Soriano were guys who didn't have to work at it as hard, but they were so naturally gifted.

Of course, there were dozens of players who have proven you don't have to be a tremendous athlete to be a great player. Baseball is one of the few sports where that's possible.

Technically, some players are genetically gifted with fast-twitch muscle fibers, which promotes capability to generate force over a given period of time. This force in baseball action includes bat speed through the hitting zone, running speed on the base paths, and arm speed for pitching and/or throwing from their position. The other area necessary for on-field success is centered on the skill level. These skills include hand-eye coordination, visual tracking of the baseball, and the ability to read the path of a ground ball or fly ball. Players that reach and achieve success at the major league level have some combination of athleticism and skill level.

When Williams was signed back in the '80s, he weighed probably 170-180 pounds—if that. He was still a kid, a teenager, who was more into track at the time instead of baseball. He had a cast on one of his wrists, glasses, and I'm thinking, *This is a big-time prospect with the Yankees?*

When Williams first came to Yankee Stadium, I know Winfield spoke with him quite a bit. Williams really respected and adored Winfield so much and wanted to carry on that sort of example that Winfield set and become the kind of player and person he was. That was the first time I remember meeting Williams. When I got back to the Yankees years later, he was a totally different player, physically and emotionally. He had grown into his body and into the player and person Yankees fans now revere.

As a strength and conditioning coach, I could tell when a player was slowing down. You could see the physical difference in them at the latter part of their careers, when they were just about at the end. You can tell by the nagging injuries and the constant muscle soreness, their inability to bounce back from competition and from the daily grind. I also had the concrete evidence of the stopwatch or measuring a vertical jump, their ability to produce power or speed. That's something that cannot be argued. Scouts will say it looks like someone lost a step on the bases or going to the shortstop hole. Plays that someone used to make almost automatically can't be accomplished regularly anymore. Even if it's a small subtlety, you can tell the difference when it's just about time to go. You can see the strain on someone's face. There's a saying from an old country song by Toby Keith: "I ain't as good as I once was, but I'm good once as I ever was."

Even top players slow down, but every now and then they're going to have a hell of a game. That was true of all those guys from our former championship teams, but maybe those moments weren't as frequent as they once were. Randy Johnson was another prime example of that thinking. Like with Doc Gooden throwing his no-hitter for the Yankees in 1996, every once in a while, you're going to get a throwback performance. We acquired the five-time Cy Young Award winner on New Year's Eve of 2004 in a deal that sent Javier Vazquez as the main piece of our three-player package to the Arizona Diamondbacks.

I've talked a lot about guys who were uncomfortable in New York, and the Big Unit clearly did not like it there from the start. He got into an argument with a TV cameraman outside his hotel the first day he arrived in town. The 6'10" Johnson had a very surly personality. He had a scowl on his face to begin with. You'd say something to him, and he was not too quick to answer—if he looked at you at all. Or he'd often look at you sideways.

Right from the beginning, he didn't understand New York, the media, the demands of playing there as a star player. Two years later we traded him back to the Diamondbacks.

Like with every new player, the training staff pored over Johnson's medical history. We adjusted and accommodated to any player and then sat down to discuss it with them. I also would contact the strength and conditioning coaches from his previous teams. With Johnson it was about trying to take care of his knees, his back, and keeping those parts strong without aggravating them further. Johnson was a very challenging athlete to train because he was so tall, so long-limbed, at an advanced age, and had so many miles on him.

It wasn't a matter of trying to recreate the wheel at all. It was trying to figure out what he was comfortable doing from a physical standpoint. He had tremendous success in his Hall of Fame career, and I wanted him to be able to carry that on with whatever physical activity he was comfortable with doing. It wasn't a lack of effort with him. He would make all of his starts, and we would perform a regular workout routine. I think he really wanted to succeed in New York. With our lineup all you had to do was give up three or four runs in six or seven innings and you would rack up wins. Even in what were not considered peak years for him, he won 17 games in each of his two seasons with us.

Tony Womack, one of Johnson's former Diamondbacks teammates and a central figure in the game-winning rally in Game 7 for Arizona in the 2001 World Series, also was signed by the Yankees for 2005. He turned out to be little more than a placeholder for our next great homegrown player. In previous spring trainings, whenever we would have meetings in Tampa, Florida, of all the projected players coming up through the system, Mark Newman and his staff always raved about Robinson Cano. You heard very little negative talk about him from anyone in the organization. He could help the team win with both his bat and his glove. He was extremely polished on both sides of the ball even at a young age. He had huge upside. The first time I saw him take batting practice, you could see the ball jumping off his bat. He hit bombs and he also hit line drives all over the field. I remember telling my friends in the New York/New Jersey area that Cano was going to be a perennial .300 hitter and 30-homer star. He had such a sweet swing and he was so smooth around second base. There was a difference from other players because the ball just carried like crazy off his bat.

Another notable thing about Cano is that the Texas Rangers had a choice of a few of our prospects as the player to be named later, in addition to Soriano, in the Alex Rodriguez trade.

Cano was included on that list, but Texas bypassed him and took an infielder named Joaquin Arias instead. Man, imagine if they'd gotten both Soriano and Cano. It was like Walter Payton or Jerry Rice being passed up in NFL drafts.

Throughout his career Cano was sometimes singled out for not hustling hard on the bases. He did have a laissez-faire personality at times, but what a talent he was. He'd play catch with A-Rod to warm up before games, and one of them would stand by the on-deck circle, and the other one would be all the way down in the right-field corner. Cano could throw it that full distance with that underarm sling throw of his. It was strange to see but amazing. His throws would be right on the money, covering about 300 feet or 100 yards.

I'm not surprised with anyone when it comes to performance-enhancing drugs. Still I could say I was slightly caught off guard—or at least more so than with some other guys who got popped over the years—when Cano was suspended for testing positive in 2018 while he was with the Seattle Mariners. As their careers advanced, some of these guys tried to maintain certain levels of success. If they're not doing it through hard work, they're possibly going to take a shortcut or get talked into it somehow. As you get older, you feel like you're losing a step, or injuries have added up over the years. You might want to take the quick way out to try to maintain the level that you've set for yourself. Recuperation also is a big key along with the ability for the muscles to heal and to be able to perform again.

Womack was totally unproductive in the first couple of months in 2005, and the organization knew it was time to bring up Cano. We definitely needed a spark. Second base was like a black hole for a couple of years after Soriano was traded. That team was lacking athleticism and team speed.

We also needed to replenish our starting pitching again beyond Johnson's arrival, which brings me to Carl Pavano, who turned out to be one of the worst free-agent signings in team history. Pavano, a member of the 2003 Florida Marlins team that beat us in the World Series, endured all sorts of nagging injuries from the time he arrived. He would make an effort. He was a consistent worker, but he would fall apart from these little muscular injuries. He'd be close to getting healthy from a stretch on the disabled list and then he'd pull another muscle. The strained glute was the one that kind of sent him over the edge. George King of the *New York Post* even coined the fitting nickname "American Idle," and guys actually used to call Pavano that. Derek Jeter and Jorge Posada would rib him and say, "Hey, Idle."

I don't think Pavano was afraid of New York at all. He just couldn't ever get on the mound. He pitched well in the World Series against us. He won 18 games in 2004 for the Marlins and he'd been durable, throwing more than 200 innings. He had a big frame, a good fastball, and a good breaking ball. It just never worked out for him. He made 26 starts over the course of a four-year, $39.95 million contract.

We also added Jaret Wright, the former Cleveland Indians ace, in 2005. After reaching Game 7 of the ALCS the year before, we went out and got three new starting pitchers: Johnson, Pavano, and Wright. The last two especially didn't work out at all. Johnson pitched decently even if he wasn't the Johnson of old. By midseason because of various injuries, we had to make more changes to the rotation. One reason we ended up winning the AL East was because of Aaron Small coming in and Chien-Ming Wang getting summoned from the minors. Small was so happy to be there and have a chance to pitch in the majors. We scored a lot of runs when he pitched, but he went 10–0 with a 3.20 ERA in the second half. He truly came out of nowhere. He'd pitched only eight games in the majors over the previous six years due to injuries. He pitched unbelievably well down the stretch.

Wang and I were tight right way. I loved to work with this guy and vice versa. He was one of my favorites. He wanted to be good and to throw hard and he worked so hard to do so. He would do anything I suggested and he felt good about it. It was just really positive feedback. He was a bulldog and a big guy built like Don Drysdale or Roger Clemens. He threw such a heavy ball, that hard sinker. He got so many double plays because of it. Wang was so different from pitchers you see now because he hardly struck anyone out. It mostly was pitch after pitch getting pounded into the ground. Even the next year in 2006, when he won 19 games for the first of back-to-back seasons, he only struck out 76 batters in more than 200 innings. You don't see that anymore. Hitters would say it was like swinging and hitting the fender of your car. Wang tore ankle ligaments running the bases in Houston while having to bat in an interleague game against the Astros in 2008. His career never was the same. He was 54–20 in his first four seasons with the Yankees before he got injured, but he only won 14 games the remainder of his career.

Those last couple of years, there also were some coaching staff changes. Willie Randolph was hired by the New York Mets after the

2004 season, and Larry Bowa replaced him. Don Mattingly also came back as our hitting coach, which was very cool for me and a lot of fans of the team. Mattingly later worked as Joe Torre's bench coach in Los Angeles after the latter's departure from New York following the 2007 season. Mattingly went on to finally get his first managerial shot with the Dodgers in 2011 and he moved on to the renamed Miami Marlins—with Jeter as a part-owner and the head of baseball operations—in 2016.

In 2005 we also had the rare opportunity to play at Busch Stadium in St. Louis, which was so fun for me since I listened to all of those Cardinals games while growing up in Iowa.

On Sunday afternoon word started spreading that we were going to shut down batting practice early because Stan Musial was in our locker room. I'm sure his presence was due to Torre knowing him going back to his days in St. Louis, but there was Stan the Man sitting on a barstool in the middle of the clubhouse. It was a sight to see. Everyone was giving him a ball to sign. I'd never seen players lined up like that. It was like people getting ready to go into confession or getting in line to board an airplane. Just to shake his hand, have a short word, and get a ball signed was a really special moment for me.

Going back a few years, I felt the same when we played at Wrigley Field in 2003. In all my years with the Yankees, we only played there once. Jeter had just been named captain by George Steinbrenner—the first Yankees captain since Mattingly retired—while we were in Cincinnati. We moved on to Chicago, which I'd traveled to with my dad to see the Cardinals face the Cubs as a young boy. That was nostalgic for me to be on the field and in the dugout with the Yankees. Wrigley Field, Yankee Stadium, and Fenway Park all have that different feeling of energy because the fans are right on top of you and they also have such rich traditions.

A-Rod actually had a monster year in 2005, winning the first of his AL MVP awards for the Yankees, hitting .321 with 48 homers and 130 RBIs. Of course, he didn't produce in the postseason in either 2005 against the Los Angeles Angels or in 2006 against the Detroit Tigers, going a combined 3-for-29 in two first-round knockouts after actually faring pretty well in his first October with us in 2004. You could see in the postseason that he looked so different at the plate, rarely looking comfortable. You almost thought to yourself, *Oh man, here we go again.* It's like he was almost fishing up there to try to hit.

With Gary Sheffield injured in 2006, we added another very professional hitter to our lineup in Bobby Abreu via a trade with the Philadelphia Phillies. After his first game at Yankee Stadium, a few of us were down in the weight room, and Abreu came in saying he wanted to lift and ride the bike for a while. Usually after a game guys are in there for no more than 20 minutes, but time was really passing by. I remember thinking to myself, *What is this?* I was just getting to know this player and his work ethic and routine. He said to me, "Do you think the reporters are gone by now?"

Someone came in and said they were all gone, and Abreu returned to the clubhouse. He had stayed down there to avoid the press, and I thought this was not a good start, considering he was in New York. Abreu, though, could really hit against righties or lefties, drew a lot of walks, and fouled off a lot of pitches. He was a totally professional hitter, and I know Bowa was a big supporter from their days together in Philadelphia. With Abreu manning right field, Torre shoehorned Shef's powerful bat into the lineup by using him at first base when he returned from the disabled list late in the season.

That first-round loss to the Tigers in '06 was a particularly rough one. Steinbrenner was pissed at Torre, and a few of the papers actually wrote that The Boss was going to make a change. A slumping A-Rod even was dropped to eighth in the lineup for Game 4 of that series.

Torre stayed on for one more year, but I was one of a handful of people in the organization who was let go after the season. That season never was comfortable. There never was that full-bore feeling. It was almost two steps forward, one step back, as we brought in different big-name players who didn't live up to the level of what the previous group did.

Nothing went smoothly those last two years, and it was heightened by imperfect chemistry. There were so many moving parts beyond the few core guys who still were there and so many new pieces at key positions. Everything seemed forced. You could tell that it was a totally different situation than the years when we were winning. I was contacted by Brian Cashman soon after the season ended. Our meeting didn't last long. I drove into Yankee Stadium, and Cash told me they were going to make a change. I also remember him saying there are people who are going to be here long after we were gone who were making these decisions.

I don't know if this decision was based on players, administration, or ownership. Cash didn't really say anything related to my job performance that was concrete or pinpointed. It was more of an open-ended, we-want-to-make-a-change conversation, the old difference in philosophy.

He also told me it was a done deal in case I had any ideas of trying to talk him out of it. I was done. I don't think he even said they appreciated my efforts or all my years of contributions.

There was nothing said about there being a combination of some very significant players who were tired of me. I don't know whether that happened or not. After different relationships with various personal trainers and aggravating some guys, that was a possibility if you added up all those factors.

We also hadn't won the World Series in six years, and teams in that situation make changes. I think the other possible ingredient was my closeness with Torre. He was losing his grip of power within the organization, and it certainly could have been a shot at the manager by ownership or the front office. I'm not saying that was the reason, but like David Cone said, "Mangold was one of Joe's guys." If it was perceived that way, maybe they could hurt Torre with any little jabs at his staff. Either way after nine seasons, it was time for them to get a new voice in the weight room. And it was time for me to move on from the Yankees for a second time.

Moving On
and Appreciating
the Yankees

THE 2006 SEASON WITH THE NEW YORK YANKEES TURNED OUT TO BE my final year in professional baseball. It was not for a lack of trying. I kept my ear to the ground to see if there were any openings to pursue a continuation of my career. I had a network of contacts, including Major League Baseball general managers, athletic trainers, and strength and conditioning coaches.

Admittedly, it would have taken a lot for us to uproot our family and move from our New Jersey home at that time. The kids were extremely grounded in their schools. By 2006 Sean was a 16-year-old sophomore in high school, Jaime was a freshman, and Jesse was in middle school.

I was contacting different teams, but I didn't even sniff out an interview with anyone. It was very perplexing and frustrating, to be honest.

Throughout all of my experiences in the major leagues and college sports, I also developed an idea regarding a software application for sports teams to utilize relative to electronic medical records. The program I'm working to develop would provide department heads, coaches, and administrators with key performance indicators located in one central repository. These pertinent metrics provide better information for better decisions and assist in optimizing athletic performance and reduce chance of injury.

Whether it be the testing and evaluation of the athletes, their speed, their power, their agility, their flexibility, range of motion, their medical history, the equipment that they utilize, their contact information, all of these types of data points would be in one location. Imagine being able to go back and see information on an 18-year-old Derek Jeter. This data would have size, weight, workout routine, vertical jump, and 60-yard dash time, and you could compare it to the same data throughout his career. Just to be able to benchmark successes would effectively provide helpful information for scouting departments.

For almost 14 years, I was trying to get this software off the ground, but at the same time, I was still training people and trying to get hired by another major league team. During the 2013 World Baseball Classic, I was named the strength and conditioning coach on Joe Torre's staff with Team USA. This was an exciting opportunity to represent the United States and to get back on the field again. I must admit wearing a uniform with USA on it made me proud. It also was a special honor to reconnect with Willie Randolph, an individual who has looked out for me over the course of my career. Randolph was a member of Torre's staff, along with Larry Bowa, Dale Murphy, and Greg Maddux. Gene Monahan, my longtime running mate with the Yankees, served as the athletic trainer.

In 2012 I also began working with a friend of mine who owns a logistics company, dealing with trucking freights across the country. I kind of had been spinning my wheels working early mornings, training clients every morning of the week Monday through Saturday and then also working in Fairlawn, New Jersey, with this company called Ultra Logistics. The gentleman who owns the company was one of the people I trained in the mornings. I've trained him for 25 years. I'd often train people at their homes—not at a gym or any sort of training facility.

I didn't get any nibbles from any major league teams in those years, and that was very frustrating. I feel like I have more in the tank with my health and fitness and my knowledge.

It was very perplexing at the end with the Yankees when I did not get re-signed. Perhaps I had worn out my welcome over nine years, following a five-year stint in the '80s. Sometimes a new face or a new voice is needed, but I did not believe that was the case with us. I don't know if I rubbed a couple of people the wrong way. I think back to my initial goals of motivating the players and implementing a sports-specific training program with the Yankees. On top of that, I had to deal with various personal trainers who were interjecting their philosophies and their thoughts on various players.

It would have been understandable on my end to push back, but I tried not to do that. I was hired to do a job, hired to train and keep these players healthy, to optimize performance, and to prevent injury. To have these other voices in the players' ears all the time was not easy. Whether people knew what was happening or not, I believe the guilt-by-association of me being in that position at the same time as prominent performance-enhancing-drug-stained players like Roger Clemens, Jason Giambi, Alex Rodriguez, and others probably hurt my prospect of getting another job in baseball. I do believe that. It was such a bombshell topic that I think I got hit with shrapnel. Quite a few people probably did. I think people seeing even an association with Clemens' personal trainer, Brian McNamee, led to a situation of other teams saying, "Jeff, we don't even want to touch that."

If you're associated with any of that, it's almost like you're viewed as toxic because of the fact you were there at the same time. No other team ever expressed that to me specifically in the subsequent years.

No one ever said, "Look, even if you weren't involved, we can't hire you."

Even if another job in baseball does not come to fruition, I've been incredibly fortunate.

I don't know if it was simply the luck of the draw or it was predetermined by a higher level, but for a small-town kid from Iowa to work for the New York Yankees—and it's nothing against the Cincinnati Reds or the Kansas City Royals or even the Mets, but we're talking about the pinnacle of sports with the Yankees—is unbelievable. I was thinking about this. It's like being a priest and instead of some small dioceses for your first job, some small church, I went right to Rome. I basically jumped over about 10 rungs on the ladder in one leap. It was just the daily excitement of it. I told Torre multiple times when he'd be working out with me, "Joe, this is the greatest job around. I'm so lucky to do this."

It was just fabulous. You can't help yourself but to think that. He would nod his head and agree, as if to acknowledge how special it was to do what we did and work where we worked every day. Another tremendous aspect of working with the Yankees—and this could be with any team in MLB but especially with them— you had the ability to win every day and every year. You got to compete every day. What's so unique about baseball is they play that national anthem every day, and it's time to go. Football is once a week. Basketball is maybe three or four times a week, and hockey is the same. Baseball is usually six days out of seven and sometimes seven out of seven. The emotions—to win or lose—are there every day. I think back to postgame workouts for guys. Either they were exhilarated from winning or they were pissed off and upset about losing. Either way there's still adrenaline flowing and emotion. It's addictive.

I can't even sum up the seat that I had for so many important moments in baseball history. The period of my life from being 29 years old until I was 50 was amazing. The Yankees were a traveling circus at times, but to be a part of such a revered organization, a team that people loved, but also loved to hate, was incredible. I liked going on the road and seeing people coming out to boo us because it also meant they wanted to see you. Deep down they respected you.

What are the chances of me flying into New York City for an interview on a cold 1983 winter day and being offered a job with the Yankees, the greatest organization in the history of sports? I'd always thought about New York, but I'd never even been there before. After I went back to Gainesville, Florida, having verbally agreed with Bill Bergesch to accept the position, I remember being in an office all by myself near the weight room at the University of Florida. I hung up the phone, stood up, and declared, "God damn, I'm a New York Yankee."

Gene Coleman of the Houston Astros was probably the first strength and conditioning coach in professional baseball, but he didn't travel with the team. I was the first to be a full-time member of a team's staff, part of their regular traveling party. Just to see the changes in philosophy, the changes in facilities, the changes in acceptance regarding the importance of strength and conditioning for baseball and to break the barrier of what people thought of it is something that fills me with pride.

As someone who is so passionate about the strength and conditioning side of it, it doesn't bother me when people talk about the steroids era. A lot of fans got turned off by it, and it affected a lot of people's legacies in the game from that era. I believe MLB was right to implement testing for PEDs. The dark cloud over that period left a stain on the game. MLB took too long in addressing it. I don't know if it was the Major League Baseball Players' Association or the owners, but there was so much money involved, and it got away from everyone on both sides of the equation.

The silver lining of getting let go by the Yankees was my opportunity to witness my children in their own competitions—Sean playing three high school sports and then college football, Jaime running cross country and track as a Division I NCAA student-athlete, and Jesse in cross country and academic decathlon, while also graduating as valedictorian of his high school class. It made up for all that I had missed during my MLB career.

My prized possessions from my time in baseball mostly were the intangible aspects of the respect factor from players and coaching staffs—both with the teams you worked for and from other teams. To listen to players and to gain their trust was something special. They could tell me anything. I enjoyed being a sounding board for them. I always tried to eliminate doubt, to build their confidence, to tell them not to give up and keep working. These are some of the marquee athletes of all time, so to have them value my opinion was very rewarding.

So many players say the toughest part is walking away, and it was tough to walk away from the locker room, the camaraderie, the airplane flights, the big games, the relationships. That's an experience that very few people get to live out. I haven't ever taken it for granted.

During many nights of flying across the country at all hours of the night, I'd sit by the window and look at the stars and the clouds and the lights below and think to myself, *This is incredible.*

I truly couldn't believe I got to be a part of it, and it's something that no one ever can take away from me—the pride and power of the pinstripes.

Acknowledgments

TO MY LOVELY WIFE, GALE, FOR HAVING UNWAVERING FAITH IN ME and encouraging me to pursue my passion. For allowing the long stretches of time for me to be away from you as you directed our family through the incredible highs and gut-wrenching lows of life. You are a true companion and have gone far beyond as a partner and as a mother helping to raise our children.

To our three children—Sean, Jaime, and Jesse—who shared many of your athletic and academic successes with a father not physically present during important moments in your lives during baseball season. Being your father is truly my pride and joy. The many gifts each of you possess makes us a great team.

With gratitude to my brothers Greg and Mark and my sisters Cathy, Chris, and Karen for always being supportive and dedicated fans.

A special memory of my mom and dad, Frank and Margaret Mangold, for their pride and confidence in me by not raising an eyebrow when I told them I wanted to do something different with my life.

In memory of our beautiful daughter Shannon. You taught me when tested to endure with faith and to value every day whether we win or lose.

A special thank you to Bill Ames and editor Jeff Fedotin of Triumph Books for having the faith in me and providing the platform for this book and helping us reach the finish line. This book could not have been written without the tireless effort of Peter Botte, who assembled my stories and thoughts into the words on these pages.

A special thank you to the incomparable Mariano Rivera, the greatest closer in baseball history and a good friend, for his incredibly thoughtful insights in writing the foreword. To longtime friend Joe Carretta, who has mentored and taught me to never accept defeat. He encouraged me to expand as an entrepreneur and demonstrated admirable wisdom and resilience in business. He encouraged me to start my own business and document my career experiences in this book.

To Boyd Epley and Mike Arthur, Nebraska Cornhuskers and early pioneers and leaders in the strength and conditioning arena for optimizing athletic performance. They each took the time to mentor me early in my career and built the foundation of training principles that set the stage for my career as a strength coach.

To Rich Tuten and the University of Florida athletic department for hiring me to my first full-time position.

To the late George Steinbrenner, who had the foresight to recognize the need for incorporating strength and conditioning into the world of Major League Baseball in 1984 and for making me the first strength and conditioning coach in this field, proving to be an innovator, not an imitator.

My two childhood athletic heroes from Omaha, Nebraska, Gale Sayers and Bob Gibson. I was inspired by them in my youth, listening on the radio or watching on television, as they demonstrated their athleticism and fierce, competitive drive to win.

Longtime player, coach, and manager Willie Randolph, with whom I shared many major league highlights and special moments. Willie stepped forward on my behalf on several career moves, including my years with the New York Yankees, New York Mets, and Team USA Baseball. Longtime athletic trainer Gene Monahan for his professionalism and support as a friend within the Yankees' medical staff.

To the many athletes I had the opportunity to work with through my career to support them and to optimize their performance on the field. Finally, I'm grateful to have had the opportunity to work alongside some of the biggest names in Major League Baseball, regarding players and managers. Joe Torre had the most impact as a manager on our Yankees championships teams, and I was honored to be a part of his staff. I revered his leadership style and learned many lessons on how to bring out the best in the players. Joe demonstrated exemplary leadership and empathy but always held a firm and steady hand as "Skipper" of our team.

Sources

Books

Appel, Marty, *Pinstripe Empire: The New York Yankees from Before the Babe to After the Boss*, Bloomsbury USA (2012).

Botte, Peter, *The Big 50: New York Yankees: The Men and Moments That Made the New York Yankees*, Triumph Books (2019).

Cone, David and Curry, Jack, *Full Count: The Education of a Pitcher*, Grand Central Publishing (2019).

Madden, Bill, *Steinbrenner: The Last Lion of Baseball*, Harper Collins Publishing (2010).

Olney, Buster, *The Last Night of the Yankees Dynasty*, Harper Perennial (2005).

Roberts, Selena, *A-Rod: The Many Lives of Alex Rodriguez*, Harper (2009).

Torre, Joe and Verducci, Tom, *The Yankee Years* (2008).

Wells, David, *Perfect I'm Not: Boomer on Beer, Brawls, Backaches, and Baseball*, William Morrow (2003).

Periodicals

Newsday
New York Daily News
New York Post
Lincoln Journal Star
Los Angeles Times
Sioux City Journal
Sports Illustrated
Sport magazine
Tallahassee Democrat
The (Cedar Rapids, Iowa,) Gazette
The (Newark, New Jersey,) Star-Ledger
The New York Times

Websites

baseball-reference.com
espn.com
mlb.com
sabr.org
yankees.com
yesnetwork.com